C-998

CAREER EXAMINATION

THIS IS YOUR **PASSBOOK**® FOR ...

SENIOR CIVIL ENGINEER

NLC®

NATIONAL LEARNING CORPORATION®
passbooks.com

COPYRIGHT NOTICE

This book is SOLELY intended for, is sold ONLY to, and its use is RESTRICTED to individual, bona fide applicants or candidates who qualify by virtue of having seriously filed applications for appropriate license, certificate, professional and/or promotional advancement, higher school matriculation, scholarship, or other legitimate requirements of educational and/or governmental authorities.

This book is NOT intended for use, class instruction, tutoring, training, duplication, copying, reprinting, excerption, or adaptation, etc., by:

1) Other publishers
2) Proprietors and/or Instructors of «Coaching» and/or Preparatory Courses
3) Personnel and/or Training Divisions of commercial, industrial, and governmental organizations
4) Schools, colleges, or universities and/or their departments and staffs, including teachers and other personnel
5) Testing Agencies or Bureaus
6) Study groups which seek by the purchase of a single volume to copy and/or duplicate and/or adapt this material for use by the group as a whole without having purchased individual volumes for each of the members of the group
7) Et al.

Such persons would be in violation of appropriate Federal and State statutes.

PROVISION OF LICENSING AGREEMENTS. — Recognized educational, commercial, industrial, and governmental institutions and organizations, and others legitimately engaged in educational pursuits, including training, testing, and measurement activities, may address request for a licensing agreement to the copyright owners, who will determine whether, and under what conditions, including fees and charges, the materials in this book may be used them. In other words, a licensing facility exists for the legitimate use of the material in this book on other than an individual basis. However, it is asseverated and affirmed here that the material in this book CANNOT be used without the receipt of the express permission of such a licensing agreement from the Publishers. Inquiries re licensing should be addressed to the company, attention rights and permissions department.

All rights reserved, including the right of reproduction in whole or in part, in any form or by any means, electronic or mechanical, including photocopying, recording, or by any information storage and retrieval system, without permission in writing from the Publisher.

Copyright © 2020 by

NLC®

National Learning Corporation

212 Michael Drive, Syosset, NY 11791
(516) 921-8888 • www.passbooks.com
E-mail: info@passbooks.com

PUBLISHED IN THE UNITED STATES OF AMERICA

PASSBOOK® SERIES

THE *PASSBOOK® SERIES* has been created to prepare applicants and candidates for the ultimate academic battlefield – the examination room.

At some time in our lives, each and every one of us may be required to take an examination – for validation, matriculation, admission, qualification, registration, certification, or licensure.

Based on the assumption that every applicant or candidate has met the basic formal educational standards, has taken the required number of courses, and read the necessary texts, the *PASSBOOK® SERIES* furnishes the one special preparation which may assure passing with confidence, instead of failing with insecurity. Examination questions – together with answers – are furnished as the basic vehicle for study so that the mysteries of the examination and its compounding difficulties may be eliminated or diminished by a sure method.

This book is meant to help you pass your examination provided that you qualify and are serious in your objective.

The entire field is reviewed through the huge store of content information which is succinctly presented through a provocative and challenging approach – the question-and-answer method.

A climate of success is established by furnishing the correct answers at the end of each test.

You soon learn to recognize types of questions, forms of questions, and patterns of questioning. You may even begin to anticipate expected outcomes.

You perceive that many questions are repeated or adapted so that you can gain acute insights, which may enable you to score many sure points.

You learn how to confront new questions, or types of questions, and to attack them confidently and work out the correct answers.

You note objectives and emphases, and recognize pitfalls and dangers, so that you may make positive educational adjustments.

Moreover, you are kept fully informed in relation to new concepts, methods, practices, and directions in the field.

You discover that you arre actually taking the examination all the time: you are preparing for the examination by "taking" an examination, not by reading extraneous and/or supererogatory textbooks.

In short, this PASSBOOK®, used directedly, should be an important factor in helping you to pass your test.

HOW TO TAKE A TEST

I. YOU MUST PASS AN EXAMINATION

A. WHAT EVERY CANDIDATE SHOULD KNOW

Examination applicants often ask us for help in preparing for the written test. What can I study in advance? What kinds of questions will be asked? How will the test be given? How will the papers be graded?

As an applicant for a civil service examination, you may be wondering about some of these things. Our purpose here is to suggest effective methods of advance study and to describe civil service examinations.

Your chances for success on this examination can be increased if you know how to prepare. Those "pre-examination jitters" can be reduced if you know what to expect. You can even experience an adventure in good citizenship if you know why civil service exams are given.

B. WHY ARE CIVIL SERVICE EXAMINATIONS GIVEN?

Civil service examinations are important to you in two ways. As a citizen, you want public jobs filled by employees who know how to do their work. As a job seeker, you want a fair chance to compete for that job on an equal footing with other candidates. The best-known means of accomplishing this two-fold goal is the competitive examination.

Exams are widely publicized throughout the nation. They may be administered for jobs in federal, state, city, municipal, town or village governments or agencies.

Any citizen may apply, with some limitations, such as the age or residence of applicants. Your experience and education may be reviewed to see whether you meet the requirements for the particular examination. When these requirements exist, they are reasonable and applied consistently to all applicants. Thus, a competitive examination may cause you some uneasiness now, but it is your privilege and safeguard.

C. HOW ARE CIVIL SERVICE EXAMS DEVELOPED?

Examinations are carefully written by trained technicians who are specialists in the field known as "psychological measurement," in consultation with recognized authorities in the field of work that the test will cover. These experts recommend the subject matter areas or skills to be tested; only those knowledges or skills important to your success on the job are included. The most reliable books and source materials available are used as references. Together, the experts and technicians judge the difficulty level of the questions.

Test technicians know how to phrase questions so that the problem is clearly stated. Their ethics do not permit "trick" or "catch" questions. Questions may have been tried out on sample groups, or subjected to statistical analysis, to determine their usefulness.

Written tests are often used in combination with performance tests, ratings of training and experience, and oral interviews. All of these measures combine to form the best-known means of finding the right person for the right job.

II. HOW TO PASS THE WRITTEN TEST

A. NATURE OF THE EXAMINATION

To prepare intelligently for civil service examinations, you should know how they differ from school examinations you have taken. In school you were assigned certain definite pages to read or subjects to cover. The examination questions were quite detailed and usually emphasized memory. Civil service exams, on the other hand, try to discover your present ability to perform the duties of a position, plus your potentiality to learn these duties. In other words, a civil service exam attempts to predict how successful you will be. Questions cover such a broad area that they cannot be as minute and detailed as school exam questions.

In the public service similar kinds of work, or positions, are grouped together in one "class." This process is known as *position-classification*. All the positions in a class are paid according to the salary range for that class. One class title covers all of these positions, and they are all tested by the same examination.

B. FOUR BASIC STEPS

1) Study the announcement

How, then, can you know what subjects to study? Our best answer is: "Learn as much as possible about the class of positions for which you've applied." The exam will test the knowledge, skills and abilities needed to do the work.

Your most valuable source of information about the position you want is the official exam announcement. This announcement lists the training and experience qualifications. Check these standards and apply only if you come reasonably close to meeting them.

The brief description of the position in the examination announcement offers some clues to the subjects which will be tested. Think about the job itself. Review the duties in your mind. Can you perform them, or are there some in which you are rusty? Fill in the blank spots in your preparation.

Many jurisdictions preview the written test in the exam announcement by including a section called "Knowledge and Abilities Required," "Scope of the Examination," or some similar heading. Here you will find out specifically what fields will be tested.

2) Review your own background

Once you learn in general what the position is all about, and what you need to know to do the work, ask yourself which subjects you already know fairly well and which need improvement. You may wonder whether to concentrate on improving your strong areas or on building some background in your fields of weakness. When the announcement has specified "some knowledge" or "considerable knowledge," or has used adjectives like "beginning principles of..." or "advanced ... methods," you can get a clue as to the number and difficulty of questions to be asked in any given field. More questions, and hence broader coverage, would be included for those subjects which are more important in the work. Now weigh your strengths and weaknesses against the job requirements and prepare accordingly.

3) Determine the level of the position

Another way to tell how intensively you should prepare is to understand the level of the job for which you are applying. Is it the entering level? In other words, is this the position in which beginners in a field of work are hired? Or is it an intermediate or advanced level? Sometimes this is indicated by such words as "Junior" or "Senior" in the class title. Other jurisdictions use Roman numerals to designate the level – Clerk I, Clerk II, for example. The word "Supervisor" sometimes appears in the title. If the level is not indicated by the title, check the description of duties. Will you be working under very close supervision, or will you have responsibility for independent decisions in this work?

4) Choose appropriate study materials

Now that you know the subjects to be examined and the relative amount of each subject to be covered, you can choose suitable study materials. For beginning level jobs, or even advanced ones, if you have a pronounced weakness in some aspect of your training, read a modern, standard textbook in that field. Be sure it is up to date and has general coverage. Such books are normally available at your library, and the librarian will be glad to help you locate one. For entry-level positions, questions of appropriate difficulty are chosen – neither highly advanced questions, nor those too simple. Such questions require careful thought but not advanced training.

If the position for which you are applying is technical or advanced, you will read more advanced, specialized material. If you are already familiar with the basic principles of your field, elementary textbooks would waste your time. Concentrate on advanced textbooks and technical periodicals. Think through the concepts and review difficult problems in your field.

These are all general sources. You can get more ideas on your own initiative, following these leads. For example, training manuals and publications of the government agency which employs workers in your field can be useful, particularly for technical and professional positions. A letter or visit to the government department involved may result in more specific study suggestions, and certainly will provide you with a more definite idea of the exact nature of the position you are seeking.

III. KINDS OF TESTS

Tests are used for purposes other than measuring knowledge and ability to perform specified duties. For some positions, it is equally important to test ability to make adjustments to new situations or to profit from training. In others, basic mental abilities not dependent on information are essential. Questions which test these things may not appear as pertinent to the duties of the position as those which test for knowledge and information. Yet they are often highly important parts of a fair examination. For very general questions, it is almost impossible to help you direct your study efforts. What we can do is to point out some of the more common of these general abilities needed in public service positions and describe some typical questions.

1) General information

Broad, general information has been found useful for predicting job success in some kinds of work. This is tested in a variety of ways, from vocabulary lists to questions about current events. Basic background in some field of work, such as sociology or economics, may be sampled in a group of questions. Often these are principles which have become familiar to most persons through exposure rather than through formal training. It is difficult to advise you how to study for these questions; being alert to the world around you is our best suggestion.

2) Verbal ability

An example of an ability needed in many positions is verbal or language ability. Verbal ability is, in brief, the ability to use and understand words. Vocabulary and grammar tests are typical measures of this ability. Reading comprehension or paragraph interpretation questions are common in many kinds of civil service tests. You are given a paragraph of written material and asked to find its central meaning.

3) Numerical ability

Number skills can be tested by the familiar arithmetic problem, by checking paired lists of numbers to see which are alike and which are different, or by interpreting charts and graphs. In the latter test, a graph may be printed in the test booklet which you are asked to use as the basis for answering questions.

4) Observation

A popular test for law-enforcement positions is the observation test. A picture is shown to you for several minutes, then taken away. Questions about the picture test your ability to observe both details and larger elements.

5) Following directions

In many positions in the public service, the employee must be able to carry out written instructions dependably and accurately. You may be given a chart with several columns, each column listing a variety of information. The questions require you to carry out directions involving the information given in the chart.

6) Skills and aptitudes

Performance tests effectively measure some manual skills and aptitudes. When the skill is one in which you are trained, such as typing or shorthand, you can practice. These tests are often very much like those given in business school or high school courses. For many of the other skills and aptitudes, however, no short-time preparation can be made. Skills and abilities natural to you or that you have developed throughout your lifetime are being tested.

Many of the general questions just described provide all the data needed to answer the questions and ask you to use your reasoning ability to find the answers. Your best preparation for these tests, as well as for tests of facts and ideas, is to be at your physical and mental best. You, no doubt, have your own methods of getting into an exam-taking mood and keeping "in shape." The next section lists some ideas on this subject.

IV. KINDS OF QUESTIONS

Only rarely is the "essay" question, which you answer in narrative form, used in civil service tests. Civil service tests are usually of the short-answer type. Full instructions for answering these questions will be given to you at the examination. But in case this is your first experience with short-answer questions and separate answer sheets, here is what you need to know:

1) Multiple-choice Questions

Most popular of the short-answer questions is the "multiple choice" or "best answer" question. It can be used, for example, to test for factual knowledge, ability to solve problems or judgment in meeting situations found at work.

A multiple-choice question is normally one of three types—

- It can begin with an incomplete statement followed by several possible endings. You are to find the one ending which *best* completes the statement, although some of the others may not be entirely wrong.
- It can also be a complete statement in the form of a question which is answered by choosing one of the statements listed.
- It can be in the form of a problem – again you select the best answer.

Here is an example of a multiple-choice question with a discussion which should give you some clues as to the method for choosing the right answer:

When an employee has a complaint about his assignment, the action which will *best* help him overcome his difficulty is to
    A. discuss his difficulty with his coworkers
    B. take the problem to the head of the organization
    C. take the problem to the person who gave him the assignment
    D. say nothing to anyone about his complaint

In answering this question, you should study each of the choices to find which is best. Consider choice "A" – Certainly an employee may discuss his complaint with fellow employees, but no change or improvement can result, and the complaint remains unresolved. Choice "B" is a poor choice since the head of the organization probably does not know what assignment you have been given, and taking your problem to him is known as "going over the head" of the supervisor. The supervisor, or person who made the assignment, is the person who can clarify it or correct any injustice. Choice "C" is, therefore, correct. To say nothing, as in choice "D," is unwise. Supervisors have and interest in knowing the problems employees are facing, and the employee is seeking a solution to his problem.

2) True/False Questions

The "true/false" or "right/wrong" form of question is sometimes used. Here a complete statement is given. Your job is to decide whether the statement is right or wrong.

SAMPLE: A roaming cell-phone call to a nearby city costs less than a non-roaming call to a distant city.

This statement is wrong, or false, since roaming calls are more expensive.

This is not a complete list of all possible question forms, although most of the others are variations of these common types. You will always get complete directions for answering questions. Be sure you understand *how* to mark your answers – ask questions until you do.

V. RECORDING YOUR ANSWERS

Computer terminals are used more and more today for many different kinds of exams.

For an examination with very few applicants, you may be told to record your answers in the test booklet itself. Separate answer sheets are much more common. If this separate answer sheet is to be scored by machine – and this is often the case – it is highly important that you mark your answers correctly in order to get credit.

An electronic scoring machine is often used in civil service offices because of the speed with which papers can be scored. Machine-scored answer sheets must be marked with a pencil, which will be given to you. This pencil has a high graphite content which responds to the electronic scoring machine. As a matter of fact, stray dots may register as answers, so do not let your pencil rest on the answer sheet while you are pondering the correct answer. Also, if your pencil lead breaks or is otherwise defective, ask for another.

Since the answer sheet will be dropped in a slot in the scoring machine, be careful not to bend the corners or get the paper crumpled.

The answer sheet normally has five vertical columns of numbers, with 30 numbers to a column. These numbers correspond to the question numbers in your test booklet. After each number, going across the page are four or five pairs of dotted lines. These short dotted lines have small letters or numbers above them. The first two pairs may also have a "T" or "F" above the letters. This indicates that the first two pairs only are to be used if the questions are of the true-false type. If the questions are multiple choice, disregard the "T" and "F" and pay attention only to the small letters or numbers.

Answer your questions in the manner of the sample that follows:

32. The largest city in the United States is
   A. Washington, D.C.
   B. New York City
   C. Chicago
   D. Detroit
   E. San Francisco

1) Choose the answer you think is best. (New York City is the largest, so "B" is correct.)
2) Find the row of dotted lines numbered the same as the question you are answering. (Find row number 32)
3) Find the pair of dotted lines corresponding to the answer. (Find the pair of lines under the mark "B.")
4) Make a solid black mark between the dotted lines.

VI. BEFORE THE TEST

Common sense will help you find procedures to follow to get ready for an examination. Too many of us, however, overlook these sensible measures. Indeed, nervousness and fatigue have been found to be the most serious reasons why applicants fail to do their best on civil service tests. Here is a list of reminders:

- Begin your preparation early – Don't wait until the last minute to go scurrying around for books and materials or to find out what the position is all about.
- Prepare continuously – An hour a night for a week is better than an all-night cram session. This has been definitely established. What is more, a night a week for a month will return better dividends than crowding your study into a shorter period of time.
- Locate the place of the exam – You have been sent a notice telling you when and where to report for the examination. If the location is in a different town or otherwise unfamiliar to you, it would be well to inquire the best route and learn something about the building.
- Relax the night before the test – Allow your mind to rest. Do not study at all that night. Plan some mild recreation or diversion; then go to bed early and get a good night's sleep.
- Get up early enough to make a leisurely trip to the place for the test – This way unforeseen events, traffic snarls, unfamiliar buildings, etc. will not upset you.
- Dress comfortably – A written test is not a fashion show. You will be known by number and not by name, so wear something comfortable.
- Leave excess paraphernalia at home – Shopping bags and odd bundles will get in your way. You need bring only the items mentioned in the official notice you received; usually everything you need is provided. Do not bring reference books to the exam. They will only confuse those last minutes and be taken away from you when in the test room.
- Arrive somewhat ahead of time – If because of transportation schedules you must get there very early, bring a newspaper or magazine to take your mind off yourself while waiting.
- Locate the examination room – When you have found the proper room, you will be directed to the seat or part of the room where you will sit. Sometimes you are given a sheet of instructions to read while you are waiting. Do not fill out any forms until you are told to do so; just read them and be prepared.
- Relax and prepare to listen to the instructions
- If you have any physical problem that may keep you from doing your best, be sure to tell the test administrator. If you are sick or in poor health, you really cannot do your best on the exam. You can come back and take the test some other time.

VII. AT THE TEST

The day of the test is here and you have the test booklet in your hand. The temptation to get going is very strong. Caution! There is more to success than knowing the right answers. You must know how to identify your papers and understand variations in the type of short-answer question used in this particular examination. Follow these suggestions for maximum results from your efforts:

1) Cooperate with the monitor

The test administrator has a duty to create a situation in which you can be as much at ease as possible. He will give instructions, tell you when to begin, check to see that you are marking your answer sheet correctly, and so on. He is not there to guard you, although he will see that your competitors do not take unfair advantage. He wants to help you do your best.

2) Listen to all instructions

Don't jump the gun! Wait until you understand all directions. In most civil service tests you get more time than you need to answer the questions. So don't be in a hurry. Read each word of instructions until you clearly understand the meaning. Study the examples, listen to all announcements and follow directions. Ask questions if you do not understand what to do.

3) Identify your papers

Civil service exams are usually identified by number only. You will be assigned a number; you must not put your name on your test papers. Be sure to copy your number correctly. Since more than one exam may be given, copy your exact examination title.

4) Plan your time

Unless you are told that a test is a "speed" or "rate of work" test, speed itself is usually not important. Time enough to answer all the questions will be provided, but this does not mean that you have all day. An overall time limit has been set. Divide the total time (in minutes) by the number of questions to determine the approximate time you have for each question.

5) Do not linger over difficult questions

If you come across a difficult question, mark it with a paper clip (useful to have along) and come back to it when you have been through the booklet. One caution if you do this – be sure to skip a number on your answer sheet as well. Check often to be sure that you have not lost your place and that you are marking in the row numbered the same as the question you are answering.

6) Read the questions

Be sure you know what the question asks! Many capable people are unsuccessful because they failed to *read* the questions correctly.

7) Answer all questions

Unless you have been instructed that a penalty will be deducted for incorrect answers, it is better to guess than to omit a question.

8) Speed tests

It is often better NOT to guess on speed tests. It has been found that on timed tests people are tempted to spend the last few seconds before time is called in marking answers at random – without even reading them – in the hope of picking up a few extra points. To discourage this practice, the instructions may warn you that your score will be "corrected" for guessing. That is, a penalty will be applied. The incorrect answers will be deducted from the correct ones, or some other penalty formula will be used.

9) Review your answers

If you finish before time is called, go back to the questions you guessed or omitted to give them further thought. Review other answers if you have time.

10) Return your test materials

If you are ready to leave before others have finished or time is called, take ALL your materials to the monitor and leave quietly. Never take any test material with you. The monitor can discover whose papers are not complete, and taking a test booklet may be grounds for disqualification.

VIII. EXAMINATION TECHNIQUES

1) Read the general instructions carefully. These are usually printed on the first page of the exam booklet. As a rule, these instructions refer to the timing of the examination; the fact that you should not start work until the signal and must stop work at a signal, etc. If there are any *special* instructions, such as a choice of questions to be answered, make sure that you note this instruction carefully.

2) When you are ready to start work on the examination, that is as soon as the signal has been given, read the instructions to each question booklet, underline any key words or phrases, such as *least, best, outline, describe* and the like. In this way you will tend to answer as requested rather than discover on reviewing your paper that you *listed without describing*, that you selected the *worst* choice rather than the *best* choice, etc.

3) If the examination is of the objective or multiple-choice type – that is, each question will also give a series of possible answers: A, B, C or D, and you are called upon to select the best answer and write the letter next to that answer on your answer paper – it is advisable to start answering each question in turn. There may be anywhere from 50 to 100 such questions in the three or four hours allotted and you can see how much time would be taken if you read through all the questions before beginning to answer any. Furthermore, if you come across a question or group of questions which you know would be difficult to answer, it would undoubtedly affect your handling of all the other questions.

4) If the examination is of the essay type and contains but a few questions, it is a moot point as to whether you should read all the questions before starting to answer any one. Of course, if you are given a choice – say five out of seven and the like – then it is essential to read all the questions so you can eliminate the two that are most difficult. If, however, you are asked to answer all the questions, there may be danger in trying to answer the easiest one first because you may find that you will spend too much time on it. The best technique is to answer the first question, then proceed to the second, etc.

5) Time your answers. Before the exam begins, write down the time it started, then add the time allowed for the examination and write down the time it must be completed, then divide the time available somewhat as follows:

- If 3-1/2 hours are allowed, that would be 210 minutes. If you have 80 objective-type questions, that would be an average of 2-1/2 minutes per question. Allow yourself no more than 2 minutes per question, or a total of 160 minutes, which will permit about 50 minutes to review.
- If for the time allotment of 210 minutes there are 7 essay questions to answer, that would average about 30 minutes a question. Give yourself only 25 minutes per question so that you have about 35 minutes to review.

6) The most important instruction is to *read each question* and make sure you know what is wanted. The second most important instruction is to *time yourself properly* so that you answer every question. The third most important instruction is to *answer every question*. Guess if you have to but include something for each question. Remember that you will receive no credit for a blank and will probably receive some credit if you write something in answer to an essay question. If you guess a letter – say "B" for a multiple-choice question – you may have guessed right. If you leave a blank as an answer to a multiple-choice question, the examiners may respect your feelings but it will not add a point to your score. Some exams may penalize you for wrong answers, so in such cases *only*, you may not want to guess unless you have some basis for your answer.

7) Suggestions
   a. Objective-type questions
      1. Examine the question booklet for proper sequence of pages and questions
      2. Read all instructions carefully
      3. Skip any question which seems too difficult; return to it after all other questions have been answered
      4. Apportion your time properly; do not spend too much time on any single question or group of questions
      5. Note and underline key words – *all, most, fewest, least, best, worst, same, opposite,* etc.
      6. Pay particular attention to negatives
      7. Note unusual option, e.g., unduly long, short, complex, different or similar in content to the body of the question
      8. Observe the use of "hedging" words – *probably, may, most likely,* etc.
      9. Make sure that your answer is put next to the same number as the question
      10. Do not second-guess unless you have good reason to believe the second answer is definitely more correct
      11. Cross out original answer if you decide another answer is more accurate; do not erase until you are ready to hand your paper in
      12. Answer all questions; guess unless instructed otherwise
      13. Leave time for review

   b. Essay questions
      1. Read each question carefully
      2. Determine exactly what is wanted. Underline key words or phrases.
      3. Decide on outline or paragraph answer

4. Include many different points and elements unless asked to develop any one or two points or elements
5. Show impartiality by giving pros and cons unless directed to select one side only
6. Make and write down any assumptions you find necessary to answer the questions
7. Watch your English, grammar, punctuation and choice of words
8. Time your answers; don't crowd material

8) Answering the essay question

Most essay questions can be answered by framing the specific response around several key words or ideas. Here are a few such key words or ideas:

M's: manpower, materials, methods, money, management
P's: purpose, program, policy, plan, procedure, practice, problems, pitfalls, personnel, public relations

   a. Six basic steps in handling problems:
      1. Preliminary plan and background development
      2. Collect information, data and facts
      3. Analyze and interpret information, data and facts
      4. Analyze and develop solutions as well as make recommendations
      5. Prepare report and sell recommendations
      6. Install recommendations and follow up effectiveness

   b. Pitfalls to avoid
      1. *Taking things for granted* – A statement of the situation does not necessarily imply that each of the elements is necessarily true; for example, a complaint may be invalid and biased so that all that can be taken for granted is that a complaint has been registered
      2. *Considering only one side of a situation* – Wherever possible, indicate several alternatives and then point out the reasons you selected the best one
      3. *Failing to indicate follow up* – Whenever your answer indicates action on your part, make certain that you will take proper follow-up action to see how successful your recommendations, procedures or actions turn out to be
      4. *Taking too long in answering any single question* – Remember to time your answers properly

IX. AFTER THE TEST

Scoring procedures differ in detail among civil service jurisdictions although the general principles are the same. Whether the papers are hand-scored or graded by machine we have described, they are nearly always graded by number. That is, the person who marks the paper knows only the number – never the name – of the applicant. Not until all the papers have been graded will they be matched with names. If other tests, such as training and experience or oral interview ratings have been given, scores will be combined. Different parts of the examination usually have different weights. For example, the written test might count 60 percent of the final grade, and a rating of training and experience 40 percent. In many jurisdictions, veterans will have a certain number of points added to their grades.

After the final grade has been determined, the names are placed in grade order and an eligible list is established. There are various methods for resolving ties between those who get the same final grade – probably the most common is to place first the name of the person whose application was received first. Job offers are made from the eligible list in the order the names appear on it. You will be notified of your grade and your rank as soon as all these computations have been made. This will be done as rapidly as possible.

People who are found to meet the requirements in the announcement are called "eligibles." Their names are put on a list of eligible candidates. An eligible's chances of getting a job depend on how high he stands on this list and how fast agencies are filling jobs from the list.

When a job is to be filled from a list of eligibles, the agency asks for the names of people on the list of eligibles for that job. When the civil service commission receives this request, it sends to the agency the names of the three people highest on this list. Or, if the job to be filled has specialized requirements, the office sends the agency the names of the top three persons who meet these requirements from the general list.

The appointing officer makes a choice from among the three people whose names were sent to him. If the selected person accepts the appointment, the names of the others are put back on the list to be considered for future openings.

That is the rule in hiring from all kinds of eligible lists, whether they are for typist, carpenter, chemist, or something else. For every vacancy, the appointing officer has his choice of any one of the top three eligibles on the list. This explains why the person whose name is on top of the list sometimes does not get an appointment when some of the persons lower on the list do. If the appointing officer chooses the second or third eligible, the No. 1 eligible does not get a job at once, but stays on the list until he is appointed or the list is terminated.

X. HOW TO PASS THE INTERVIEW TEST

The examination for which you applied requires an oral interview test. You have already taken the written test and you are now being called for the interview test – the final part of the formal examination.

You may think that it is not possible to prepare for an interview test and that there are no procedures to follow during an interview. Our purpose is to point out some things you can do in advance that will help you and some good rules to follow and pitfalls to avoid while you are being interviewed.

What is an interview supposed to test?

The written examination is designed to test the technical knowledge and competence of the candidate; the oral is designed to evaluate intangible qualities, not readily measured otherwise, and to establish a list showing the relative fitness of each candidate – as measured against his competitors – for the position sought. Scoring is not on the basis of "right" and "wrong," but on a sliding scale of values ranging from "not passable" to "outstanding." As a matter of fact, it is possible to achieve a relatively low score without a single "incorrect" answer because of evident weakness in the qualities being measured.

Occasionally, an examination may consist entirely of an oral test – either an individual or a group oral. In such cases, information is sought concerning the technical knowledges and abilities of the candidate, since there has been no written examination for this purpose. More commonly, however, an oral test is used to supplement a written examination.

Who conducts interviews?
The composition of oral boards varies among different jurisdictions. In nearly all, a representative of the personnel department serves as chairman. One of the members of the board may be a representative of the department in which the candidate would work. In some cases, "outside experts" are used, and, frequently, a businessman or some other representative of the general public is asked to serve. Labor and management or other special groups may be represented. The aim is to secure the services of experts in the appropriate field.

However the board is composed, it is a good idea (and not at all improper or unethical) to ascertain in advance of the interview who the members are and what groups they represent. When you are introduced to them, you will have some idea of their backgrounds and interests, and at least you will not stutter and stammer over their names.

What should be done before the interview?
While knowledge about the board members is useful and takes some of the surprise element out of the interview, there is other preparation which is more substantive. It *is* possible to prepare for an oral interview – in several ways:

1) Keep a copy of your application and review it carefully before the interview
This may be the only document before the oral board, and the starting point of the interview. Know what education and experience you have listed there, and the sequence and dates of all of it. Sometimes the board will ask you to review the highlights of your experience for them; you should not have to hem and haw doing it.

2) Study the class specification and the examination announcement
Usually, the oral board has one or both of these to guide them. The qualities, characteristics or knowledges required by the position sought are stated in these documents. They offer valuable clues as to the nature of the oral interview. For example, if the job involves supervisory responsibilities, the announcement will usually indicate that knowledge of modern supervisory methods and the qualifications of the candidate as a supervisor will be tested. If so, you can expect such questions, frequently in the form of a hypothetical situation which you are expected to solve. NEVER go into an oral without knowledge of the duties and responsibilities of the job you seek.

3) Think through each qualification required
Try to visualize the kind of questions you would ask if you were a board member. How well could you answer them? Try especially to appraise your own knowledge and background in each area, *measured against the job sought*, and identify any areas in which you are weak. Be critical and realistic – do not flatter yourself.

4) Do some general reading in areas in which you feel you may be weak
For example, if the job involves supervision and your past experience has NOT, some general reading in supervisory methods and practices, particularly in the field of human relations, might be useful. Do NOT study agency procedures or detailed manuals. The oral board will be testing your understanding and capacity, not your memory.

5) Get a good night's sleep and watch your general health and mental attitude
You will want a clear head at the interview. Take care of a cold or any other minor ailment, and of course, no hangovers.

What should be done on the day of the interview?
Now comes the day of the interview itself. Give yourself plenty of time to get there. Plan to arrive somewhat ahead of the scheduled time, particularly if your appointment is in the fore part of the day. If a previous candidate fails to appear, the board might be ready for you a bit early. By early afternoon an oral board is almost invariably behind schedule if there are many candidates, and you may have to wait. Take along a book or magazine to read, or your application to review, but leave any extraneous material in the waiting room when you go in for your interview. In any event, relax and compose yourself.

The matter of dress is important. The board is forming impressions about you – from your experience, your manners, your attitude, and your appearance. Give your personal appearance careful attention. Dress your best, but not your flashiest. Choose conservative, appropriate clothing, and be sure it is immaculate. This is a business interview, and your appearance should indicate that you regard it as such. Besides, being well groomed and properly dressed will help boost your confidence.

Sooner or later, someone will call your name and escort you into the interview room. *This is it.* From here on you are on your own. It is too late for any more preparation. But remember, you asked for this opportunity to prove your fitness, and you are here because your request was granted.

What happens when you go in?
The usual sequence of events will be as follows: The clerk (who is often the board stenographer) will introduce you to the chairman of the oral board, who will introduce you to the other members of the board. Acknowledge the introductions before you sit down. Do not be surprised if you find a microphone facing you or a stenotypist sitting by. Oral interviews are usually recorded in the event of an appeal or other review.

Usually the chairman of the board will open the interview by reviewing the highlights of your education and work experience from your application – primarily for the benefit of the other members of the board, as well as to get the material into the record. Do not interrupt or comment unless there is an error or significant misinterpretation; if that is the case, do not hesitate. But do not quibble about insignificant matters. Also, he will usually ask you some question about your education, experience or your present job – partly to get you to start talking and to establish the interviewing "rapport." He may start the actual questioning, or turn it over to one of the other members. Frequently, each member undertakes the questioning on a particular area, one in which he is perhaps most competent, so you can expect each member to participate in the examination. Because time is limited, you may also expect some rather abrupt switches in the direction the questioning takes, so do not be upset by it. Normally, a board member will not pursue a single line of questioning unless he discovers a particular strength or weakness.

After each member has participated, the chairman will usually ask whether any member has any further questions, then will ask you if you have anything you wish to add. Unless you are expecting this question, it may floor you. Worse, it may start you off on an extended, extemporaneous speech. The board is not usually seeking more information. The question is principally to offer you a last opportunity to present further qualifications or to indicate that you have nothing to add. So, if you feel that a significant qualification or characteristic has been overlooked, it is proper to point it out in a sentence or so. Do not compliment the board on the thoroughness of their examination – they have been sketchy, and you know it. If you wish, merely say, "No thank you, I have nothing further to add." This is a point where you can "talk yourself out" of a good impression or fail to present an important bit of information. Remember, *you close the interview yourself.*

The chairman will then say, "That is all, Mr. _____, thank you." Do not be startled; the interview is over, and quicker than you think. Thank him, gather your belongings and take your leave. Save your sigh of relief for the other side of the door.

How to put your best foot forward

Throughout this entire process, you may feel that the board individually and collectively is trying to pierce your defenses, seek out your hidden weaknesses and embarrass and confuse you. Actually, this is not true. They are obliged to make an appraisal of your qualifications for the job you are seeking, and they want to see you in your best light. Remember, they must interview all candidates and a non-cooperative candidate may become a failure in spite of their best efforts to bring out his qualifications. Here are 15 suggestions that will help you:

1) Be natural – Keep your attitude confident, not cocky

If you are not confident that you can do the job, do not expect the board to be. Do not apologize for your weaknesses, try to bring out your strong points. The board is interested in a positive, not negative, presentation. Cockiness will antagonize any board member and make him wonder if you are covering up a weakness by a false show of strength.

2) Get comfortable, but don't lounge or sprawl

Sit erectly but not stiffly. A careless posture may lead the board to conclude that you are careless in other things, or at least that you are not impressed by the importance of the occasion. Either conclusion is natural, even if incorrect. Do not fuss with your clothing, a pencil or an ashtray. Your hands may occasionally be useful to emphasize a point; do not let them become a point of distraction.

3) Do not wisecrack or make small talk

This is a serious situation, and your attitude should show that you consider it as such. Further, the time of the board is limited – they do not want to waste it, and neither should you.

4) Do not exaggerate your experience or abilities

In the first place, from information in the application or other interviews and sources, the board may know more about you than you think. Secondly, you probably will not get away with it. An experienced board is rather adept at spotting such a situation, so do not take the chance.

5) If you know a board member, do not make a point of it, yet do not hide it
   Certainly you are not fooling him, and probably not the other members of the board. Do not try to take advantage of your acquaintanceship – it will probably do you little good.

6) Do not dominate the interview
   Let the board do that. They will give you the clues – do not assume that you have to do all the talking. Realize that the board has a number of questions to ask you, and do not try to take up all the interview time by showing off your extensive knowledge of the answer to the first one.

7) Be attentive
   You only have 20 minutes or so, and you should keep your attention at its sharpest throughout. When a member is addressing a problem or question to you, give him your undivided attention. Address your reply principally to him, but do not exclude the other board members.

8) Do not interrupt
   A board member may be stating a problem for you to analyze. He will ask you a question when the time comes. Let him state the problem, and wait for the question.

9) Make sure you understand the question
   Do not try to answer until you are sure what the question is. If it is not clear, restate it in your own words or ask the board member to clarify it for you. However, do not haggle about minor elements.

10) Reply promptly but not hastily
   A common entry on oral board rating sheets is "candidate responded readily," or "candidate hesitated in replies." Respond as promptly and quickly as you can, but do not jump to a hasty, ill-considered answer.

11) Do not be peremptory in your answers
   A brief answer is proper – but do not fire your answer back. That is a losing game from your point of view. The board member can probably ask questions much faster than you can answer them.

12) Do not try to create the answer you think the board member wants
   He is interested in what kind of mind you have and how it works – not in playing games. Furthermore, he can usually spot this practice and will actually grade you down on it.

13) Do not switch sides in your reply merely to agree with a board member
   Frequently, a member will take a contrary position merely to draw you out and to see if you are willing and able to defend your point of view. Do not start a debate, yet do not surrender a good position. If a position is worth taking, it is worth defending.

14) Do not be afraid to admit an error in judgment if you are shown to be wrong

The board knows that you are forced to reply without any opportunity for careful consideration. Your answer may be demonstrably wrong. If so, admit it and get on with the interview.

15) Do not dwell at length on your present job

The opening question may relate to your present assignment. Answer the question but do not go into an extended discussion. You are being examined for a *new* job, not your present one. As a matter of fact, try to phrase ALL your answers in terms of the job for which you are being examined.

Basis of Rating

Probably you will forget most of these "do's" and "don'ts" when you walk into the oral interview room. Even remembering them all will not ensure you a passing grade. Perhaps you did not have the qualifications in the first place. But remembering them will help you to put your best foot forward, without treading on the toes of the board members.

Rumor and popular opinion to the contrary notwithstanding, an oral board wants you to make the best appearance possible. They know you are under pressure – but they also want to see how you respond to it as a guide to what your reaction would be under the pressures of the job you seek. They will be influenced by the degree of poise you display, the personal traits you show and the manner in which you respond.

ABOUT THIS BOOK

This book contains tests divided into Examination Sections. Go through each test, answering every question in the margin. At the end of each test look at the answer key and check your answers. On the ones you got wrong, look at the right answer choice and learn. Do not fill in the answers first. Do not memorize the questions and answers, but understand the answer and principles involved. On your test, the questions will likely be different from the samples. Questions are changed and new ones added. If you understand these past questions you should have success with any changes that arise. Tests may consist of several types of questions. We have additional books on each subject should more study be advisable or necessary for you. Finally, the more you study, the better prepared you will be. This book is intended to be the last thing you study before you walk into the examination room. Prior study of relevant texts is also recommended. NLC publishes some of these in our Fundamental Series. Knowledge and good sense are important factors in passing your exam. Good luck also helps. So now study this Passbook, absorb the material contained within and take that knowledge into the examination. Then do your best to pass that exam.

EXAMINATION SECTION

EXAMINATION SECTION

TEST 1

DIRECTIONS: Each question or incomplete statement is followed by several suggested answers or completions. Select the one that BEST answers the question or completes the statement. *PRINT THE LETTER OF THE CORRECT ANSWER IN THE SPACE AT THE RIGHT.*

1. A mass diagram is used in water supply computations to determine the
   A. size of the area that will be flooded when a dam is built
   B. capacity of reservoir required to supply the demand for water
   C. volume of excavation required to clear the site for a reservoir
   D. rate of flow of water into a reservoir

   1.____

2. The velocity head in a pipe is equal to
   A. $\frac{v^2}{2g}$ B. $\frac{v^2}{g}$ C. $\frac{v}{2g}$ D. $\frac{v}{g}$

   2.____

3. A force of 200 lbs. and a force of 300 lbs. make an angle of 30° with each other. The value of the resultant force is, in lbs., MOST NEARLY
   A. 483   B. 48   C. 493   D. 513

   3.____

4. A chemical commonly used for coagulation in a water purification plant is
   A. alum   B. caustic ash   C. potash   D. saltpeter

   4.____

5. The consistency of a concrete mix is measured with a
   A. water meter   B. viscosimeter
   C. slump cone   D. vicat needle

   5.____

6. The term *4000 pound concrete* commonly means
   A. one cubic yard of concrete weighs approximately 4000 pounds
   B. the allowable stress in compression in the concrete is 400 lb./sq.in.
   C. the concrete has a minimum ultimate strength in compression of 4000 lb./sq.in. at 28 days
   D. the concrete can carry a bond stress of 4000 lb./sq.in.

   6.____

Questions 7-9.

DIRECTIONS: Questions 7 through 9 refer to the sketch of a reinforced concrete beam.

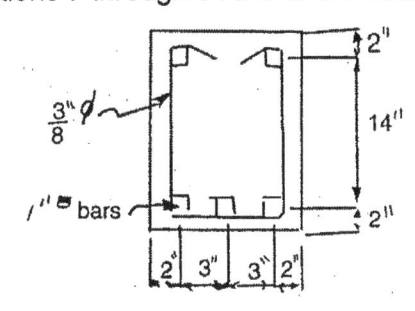

2 (#1)

7. The effective width of the beam is, in inches, MOST NEARLY
   A. 5   B. 8   C. 9   D. 10

8. The ³⁄₈" diameter bar is _____ reinforcement.
   A. temperature
   B. tension
   C. compression
   D. shear

9. Provided no 1" bars are bent up, the upper two square bars are _____ reinforcement.
   A. temperature
   B. tension
   C. compression
   D. shear

10. The sine of 120° is the same as the sine of
    A. 45°
    B. 60°
    C. 45°, but with a negative sign
    D. 60° but with a negative sign

11. The formula for the area of a triangle is
    A. ½ab sin A   B. ½bc sin A   C. ½ac cos A   D. ½ab cos A

12. The logarithm of 7 is approximately 0.845.
    The logarithm of (0.007)¼ is APPROXIMATELY
    A. 9.343-10   B. 9.567-10   C. 9.461-10   D. 9.561-10

13. The center of gravity of a triangle is located at the intersection of the
    A. angle bisectors
    B. medians
    C. perpendicular bisectors of the sides
    D. radians

14. The distance between two stations was measured six times and the average distance found to be 346.215 ft.
    If one measurement of 351.205 ft. is deleted from the data as being inconsistent with the other measurements, then the average of the remaining five measurements is, in ft.,
    A. 345.217   B. 345.221   C. 345.227   D. 345.235

15. A ma of an area 380 ft. x 740 ft. is to be plotted on a sheet of drawing paper. The SMALLEST sheet of paper required to plot this map to a scale of 1" = 50', leaving a one inch margin all around, is, in inches,
    A. 8½ x 11   B. 10 x 17   C. 12 x 17   D. 10 x 15

16. On a topographic map, widely spaced contour lines indicate
    A. a gentle slope
    B. a steep slope
    C. an overhanging cliff
    D. the bank of a stream

17. The scale to which a map is drawn is 1" = 800'.
Of the following, the MOST common method by which this scale would be indicated on the map is
A. 1/800
B. 1" = 9600"
C. 8.0" = one mile
D. 1/9600

17._____

18. The angle formed between one line and the prolongation of the preceding line in a closed traverse is known as a(n) _____ angle.
A. split
B. obtuse
C. direction
D. deflection

18._____

19. When laying out a horizontal circular curve, the deflection angle for a 100 ft. chord is equal to
A. one-quarter of the degree of curvature
B. one-half of the degree of curvature
C. three-quarters of the degree of curvature
D. the degree of curvature

19._____

20. For a given intersection angle, tables of the functions of a one degree curve show the tangent distance to be 1062.0 ft.
For the same intersection angle and a curvature of 4°, the tangent distance is, in feet, MOST NEARLY
A. 265.5
B. 437.9
C. 649.3
D. 1153.4

20._____

21. The bending moment diagram for the beam shown in the diagram at the right is
A. A
B. B
C. C
D. D

21._____

22. The bending moment at the center of a simple beam supporting a uniform load of w pounds per foot throughout its entire length, l, is
A. $\dfrac{wl^2}{2}$
B. $\dfrac{wl^2}{4}$
C. $\dfrac{3wx^2}{8}$
D. $\dfrac{wl^2}{8}$

22._____

23. A simple beam on a 16'0" span carries a concentrated load of 10,000 pounds. If the maximum bending moment in the beam is 465,000 inch pounds, the distance from the load to the nearer support is, in feet, MOST NEARLY
A. 6.1
B. 6.3
C. 6.6
D. 6.9

23._____

24. The section modulus of a rectangular beam 6 inches wide and 12 inches deep is, in inches cubed,
A. 24
B. 48
C. 96
D. 144

24._____

25. A 6" x 8" timber (actual size) is to be used as a beam on a simple span. If the 8-inch side is vertical rather than the 6-inch side, the beam is NOT
   A. stronger in bending
   B. stronger in shear
   C. stiffer
   D. more efficient

26. A 6" x 8" timber (actual size) is being used as a gin pole.
   The radius of gyration of this column which would be used in a column formula to determine safe load for the gin pole is, in inches, MOST NEARLY
   A. 1.73   B. 1.87   C. 1.93   D. 2.13

27. A steel rod 25'0" long and 1 inch square in cross-section, fastened to solid supports, is under a tension of 18,000 lb./sq.in.
   If one of the supports yields 0.14 inches, the resultant tension in the bar will be, in pounds per square inch, MOST NEARLY ($E = 30 \times 10^6$ lb./sq.in.)
   A. 3800   B. 4000   C. 4200   D. 4400

28. A round steel bar, one inch in diameter and three feet long, is elongated .022 inches by a load applied at one end of the bar.
   The magnitude of the load is, in lbs., MOST NEARLY ($E = 30 \times 10^6$ lb./sq.in.)
   A. 14,200   B. 14,400   C. 14,600   D. 14,940

29. A short hollow steel cylinder with a wall thickness of 1.5 inches is to carry a compressive load, applied uniformly on the end, of 1,750,000 lb.
   If the allowable working stress in steel in comparison is 20,000 lb./sq.in., then the minimum outside diameter of the cylinder required to safely support this load is, in inches, MOST NEARLY
   A. 19.4   B. 19.8   C. 20.0   D. 20.2

Questions 30-31.

DIRECTIONS: Questions 30 and 31 are to be answered on the basis of the following frame.

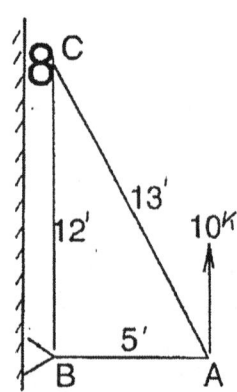

30. The reaction at joint C of the frame is, in kips, MOST NEARLY
   A. 4.17   B. 4.29   C. 4.37   D. 4.63

31. The stress in member BC of the frame is, in kips, MOST NEARLY
   A. 10.0   B. 10.6   C. 10.8   D. 11.2

32. The modulus of elasticity of aluminum is one-third that of steel. This means that
    A. steel is three times as strong as aluminum
    B. aluminum is lighter than steel
    C. aluminum is three times as strong as steel
    D. for equal stress intensities, the unit strain in aluminum is three times that in steel

32.____

Questions 33-35.

DIRECTIONS: Questions 33 through 35 are to be answered on the basis of the following stress-strain diagram.

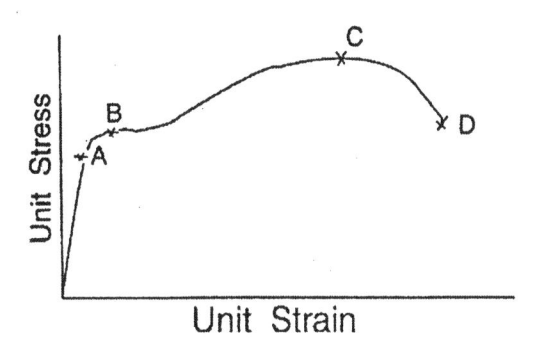

33. The stress-strain diagram is for
    A. high-carbon steel
    B. low-carbon steel
    C. cast iron
    D. concrete

33.____

34. The yield point is marked
    A. A
    B. B
    C. C
    D. D

34.____

35. The ultimate strength is marked
    A. A
    B. B
    C. C
    D. D

35.____

Questions 36-37.

DIRECTIONS: Questions 36 and 37 are to be answered on the basis of the following sketch.

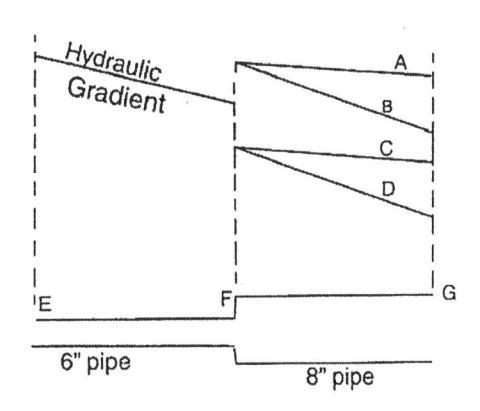

6 (#1)

36. The velocity of flow in section EF is 6'/sec.
    The velocity of flow in section FG is, in feet per second, MOST NEARLY
    A. 3.36　　B. 3.38　　C. 3.40　　D. 3.44

37. If the hydraulic gradient as shown from E to F, the hydraulic gradient from F to G is marked
    A. A　　B. B　　C. C　　D. D

38. A 6-inch pipe line is horizontal from point A to point B, the distance AB being 2000 feet. At A, the hydraulic gradient is 10 feet above the pipe; at B it is 2 feet below the pipe.
    The head lost per thousand feet is, in feet,
    A. 1　　B. 3　　C. 7　　D. 6

39. A canal is to have a cross-sectional area of 60 square feet.
    If a square cross-section is used, the hydraulic radius of the canal when flowing full will be, in feet, MOST NEARLY
    A. 2.41　　B. 2.45　　C. 2.51　　D. 2.58

40. If one cubic foot of cement weighs 94 pounds and the specific gravity of the cement particles is 3.10, the void ratio (ratio of volume of voids to volume of solids) is MOST NEARLY
    A. 0.89　　B. 0.96　　C. 1.03　　D. 1.06

KEY (CORRECT ANSWERS)

1.	B	11.	B	21.	C	31.	A
2.	A	12.	C	22.	D	32.	D
3.	A	13.	B	23.	C	33.	B
4.	A	14.	A	24.	D	34.	B
5.	C	15.	B	25.	B	35.	C
6.	C	16.	A	26.	A	36.	B
7.	D	17.	D	27.	B	37.	A
8.	D	18.	D	28.	B	38.	D
9.	C	19.	B	29.	C	39.	D
10.	B	20.	A	30.	A	40.	D

SOLUTIONS TO PROBLEMS

3. CORRECT ANSWER: A

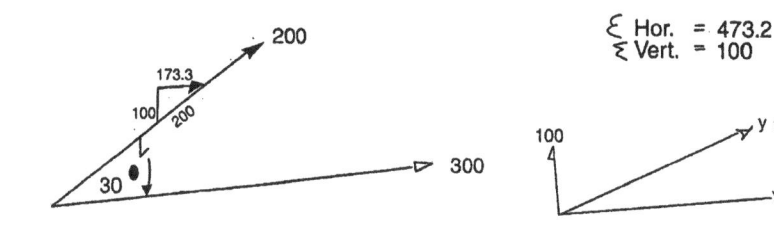

$r = \sqrt{100^2 + 473.2^2} = 483$ lbs.

10. CORRECT ANSWER: B

sin A = sin(π-A); sin 120° = sin 60°

11. CORRECT ANSWER: B

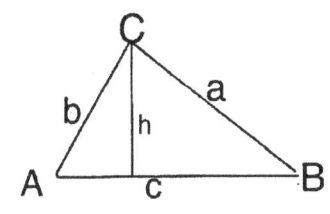

sin A = h/b
Area = $(\frac{1}{2})(c)(h) = \frac{1}{2}$bc sin A

12. CORRECT ANSWER: C

Log $(0.007)\frac{1}{4} = \frac{1}{4}$log 7 × 10^{-3} = $\frac{1}{4}$(-3+0.845) = 0.539 or 9.461-10

14. CORRECT ANSWER: A

[(6)(346.215) – 351.205]/5 = 1826.085/5 = 365.217

15. CORRECT ANSWER: A
Each dimension on paper must be increased by two inches (one inch margin on each side); 380/50 ~ 8, 740/50 ~ 15 or 10 × 17

19. CORRECT ANSWER: B
Deflection angles for 100 ft. lengths are multiples of ½ degree of curvature.

20. CORRECT ANSWER: A
Since degree of curve is described by the angle subtended by a chord or arc of 100 ft. length, the tangent distance is a direct measure of the degree of curve. For 4°, (1062.0)(¼) = 265.5 ft.

8 (#1)

22. **CORRECT ANSWER: D**

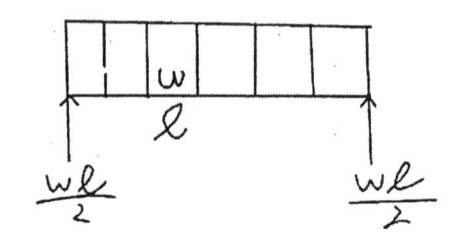

Moment @ $\frac{1}{2} = \frac{wl}{2} \frac{(1)}{(2)} - \frac{wl}{2} \frac{(1)}{(4)}$

from the rt.

$= \frac{wl^2}{4} - \frac{wl^2}{8}$

$= \frac{wl^2}{8}$

23. **CORRECT ANSWER: C**

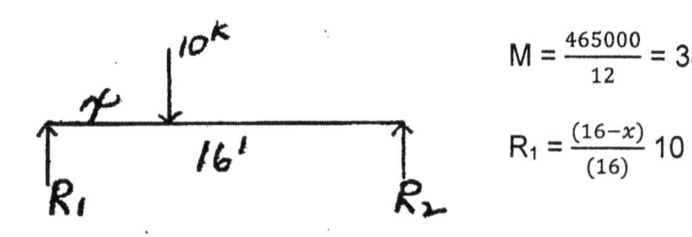

$M = \frac{465000}{12} = 38.750$ ft.-k

$R_1 = \frac{(16-x)}{(16)} 10$

$38.75 = R_1 x = \frac{(16-x)}{(16)} (10)(x) = \frac{160x - 10x^2}{16}$

$10x^2 - 160x + 38.75(16) = 0$

$x^2 - 16x + 62 = 0$

$x = \frac{-b \pm \sqrt{b^2 - 4ac}}{2a}$

$x = \frac{16 \pm \sqrt{256 - 248}}{2} = \frac{16 \pm \sqrt{8}}{2}$

$x = 8 \pm \sqrt{2}$

It must be less than 8 to be the distance to the nearer support ∴ 8 − 1.4 = 6.6

24. **CORRECT ANSWER: D**

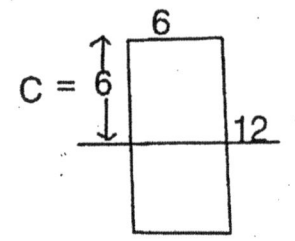

Section Modulus $= \frac{I}{c}$

$I = \frac{bh^3}{12} = \frac{6 \times 12^3}{12} = 6 \times 12^2$

$c = 6$

$\frac{I}{c} = \frac{6 \times 12^2}{6} = 12^2 = 144$

25. **CORRECT ANSWER: B**
By having the 8-inch side vertical rather than the 6-inch side, it becomes stronger in bending, stiffer and more efficient, but the shear strength remains the same.

26. **CORRECT ANSWER: A**

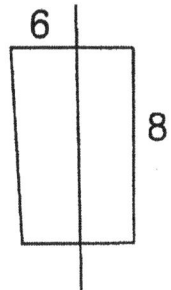

(taken about the weak axis)

$r = \dfrac{d}{\sqrt{12}}$

$d = 6$

$r = \dfrac{6}{\sqrt{12}}$ 1.73

27. **CORRECT ANSWER: B**
$E = 30 \times 10^6$
$A = \pi/4$
$\varepsilon = \dfrac{\sigma}{E} = \dfrac{18000}{30 \times 10^6} = 600 \times 10^{-6}$

Support yield = 0.14 inches = $\dfrac{0.14}{25 \times 12} = 467 \times 10^{-6}$

$(600-467) \times 10^{-6} = 133$ in/in

$\sigma = E\varepsilon = 30 \times 10^6 \times 133 \times 10^{-6} = 3990$ psi

28. **CORRECT ANSWER: B**
$E = 30 \times 10^6$ psi

$A = \dfrac{\pi D^2}{4} = \pi/4$ in^2

$\varepsilon = .022/36 = 611 \times 10^{-6}$ in/in

$\sigma = \dfrac{P}{A} = P/\pi/4$

$E = \dfrac{\sigma}{\varepsilon}$

$p = E\varepsilon \pi/4 = 30 \times 10^6 \times 611 \times 10^6 \times \pi/4 = 14{,}400$ lbs.

29. CORRECT ANSWER: C

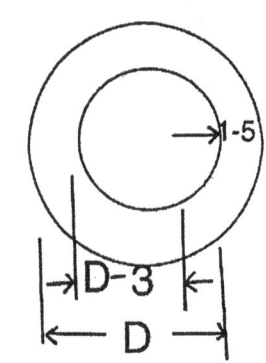

$$A = \frac{P}{\sigma} = \frac{1{,}750{,}000 \text{ lbs.}}{20{,}000 \text{ psi}} = 87.5 \text{ in}^2$$

$$\frac{\pi D^2}{4} - \frac{\pi(D-3)^2}{4} = 87.5$$

$$D^2 - (D^2 - 6D + 9) = 8.75(4/\pi)$$

$$6D = 111.4 + 9$$
$$D = 20.07$$

30. CORRECT ANSWER: A
Horizontal reaction C from ΣM about B =
C(12) = 10 × 5
C→ = 4.17

31. CORRECT ANSWER: A
ΣV = 0; BC takes only the vertical loading because of the roller at B.

32. CORRECT ANSWER: D
$$E = \frac{\sigma}{\varepsilon}$$

Steel E ≈ 30
AlE ≈ 10

$$\varepsilon_{steel} = \frac{\sigma_{const}}{30} = 1/30$$

$$\varepsilon_{al} = \frac{\sigma_{const}}{10} = 1/10$$

$$\frac{1\,al}{10} = 3\left(\frac{1st}{30}\right)$$

33. CORRECT ANSWER: B
Low carbon steel because of the ductility

36. CORRECT ANSWER: B
Q = flow (ft 3/sec.)   Q = Av
A = area(ft²)   Av = A'v
v = velocity (ft/sec)   (9π)(6) = (16π)v
                              v = 3.38

37. CORRECT ANSWER: A
The hydraulic gradient is a line drawn through a series of points to which water would rise in piezometer tubes attached to a pipe through which water flows. The head loss in the larger pipe due to friction will be at a lesser rate than the smaller pipe because of the larger diameter and lower velocity of flow.

39. CORRECT ANSWER: D

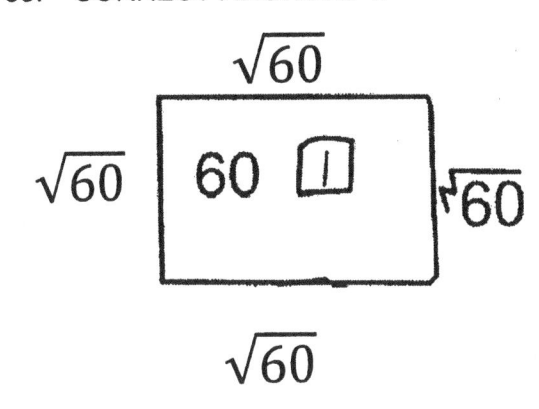

$$\text{hydraulic radius} = \frac{\text{cross-section area of water}}{\text{wetted perimeter}}$$

$$= \frac{60}{3\sqrt{60}} = 2.58$$

(Diagram: rectangle with width $\sqrt{60}$ on top and bottom, height $\sqrt{60}$ on left and right, area 60 inside)

40. CORRECT ANSWER: D
    If there were no voids, the weight of one cubic ft. would be 3.10 × 62.4 = 193.44

    Volume of voids = $\frac{193.44 - 94}{193.44}$ ft³ = $\frac{99.44}{193.44}$

    Volume of solids = $\frac{94}{193.44}$ ft³

    Void ratio = $\frac{99.44}{94.00}$ = 1.06

TEST 2

DIRECTIONS: Each question or incomplete statement is followed by several suggested answers or completions. Select the one that BEST answers the question or completes the statement. *PRINT THE LETTER OF THE CORRECT ANSWER IN THE SPACE AT THE RIGHT.*

1. A *plane table* is MOST commonly used to
   A. determine trigonometric functions of angles
   B. plot large maps in the office from data taken in the field
   C. plot maps directly in the field
   D. adjust distances from slope measurements to horizontal measurements

2. Of the following formulas used in taping, the one that gives the correction for sag is
   A. $\dfrac{h^2}{2s}$
   B. $\dfrac{0.204W\sqrt{AE}}{\sqrt{Pn-Po}}$
   C. $\dfrac{(P-Po)l}{AE}$
   D. $\dfrac{W^2L}{24P^2}$

3. Recorded distances will be less than the actual horizontal distances when measurements are taken
   A. with the tape on a slope
   B. at a temperature lower than that at which the tape was standardized
   C. with the center of the tape out of line
   D. with a tension greater than that at which the tape was standardized

4. A 100 ft. steel tape is standardized fully supported under a 10 pound pull when the temperature is 59°F and found to be 100.17 feet long. A distance of 70.00 feet is to be laid out with this tape under the standardization conditions.
   The tape distance to lay out, in feet, is
   A. 69.88   B. 69.99   C. 70.01   D. 70.12

5. In the closed traverse ABC, the bearings of lines AB and BC are N45°-00'E and N60°00'E, respectively. The lengths of these lines are 200 ft. and 300 ft., respectively. The bearing of line CA is MOST NEARLY
   A. S54°-00'W   B. S56°-00'W   C. S58°-00'W   D. S60°-00'W

6. A transit is so designed that the stadia constant C is negligible. The stadia interval factor is 200. When the telescope if level,
   A. readings must be taken on the stadia red every 100 ft.
   B. the distance from the instrument to the rod is 100 times the difference between the readings of the upper and lower crosshairs on the rod
   C. the scale used to read the stadia rod is divided into 100 parts
   D. the difference of elevation from the instrument to the point on which the rod is held is equal to the stadia reading plus 1.00 ft.

2 (#2)

Questions 7-11.

DIRECTIONS: In Questions 7 through 11, the plan and front elevation of an object are shown on the left, and on the right are shown four figures, one of which, and only one, represents the right side elevation. Indicate the letter which represents the right side elevation.

SAMPLE QUESTION: In the sample shown below, which figure correctly represents the right side elevation?

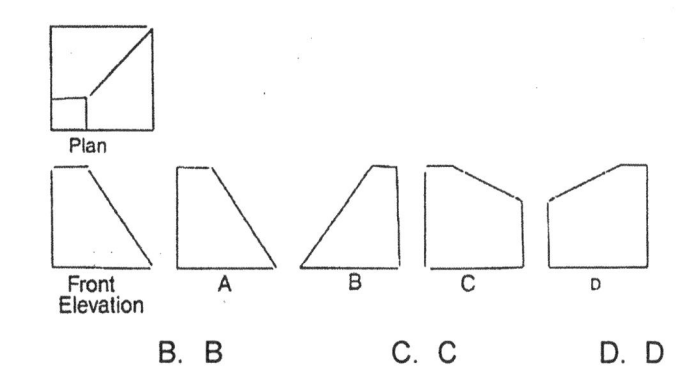

A. A B. B C. C D. D

The correct answer is A.

7.

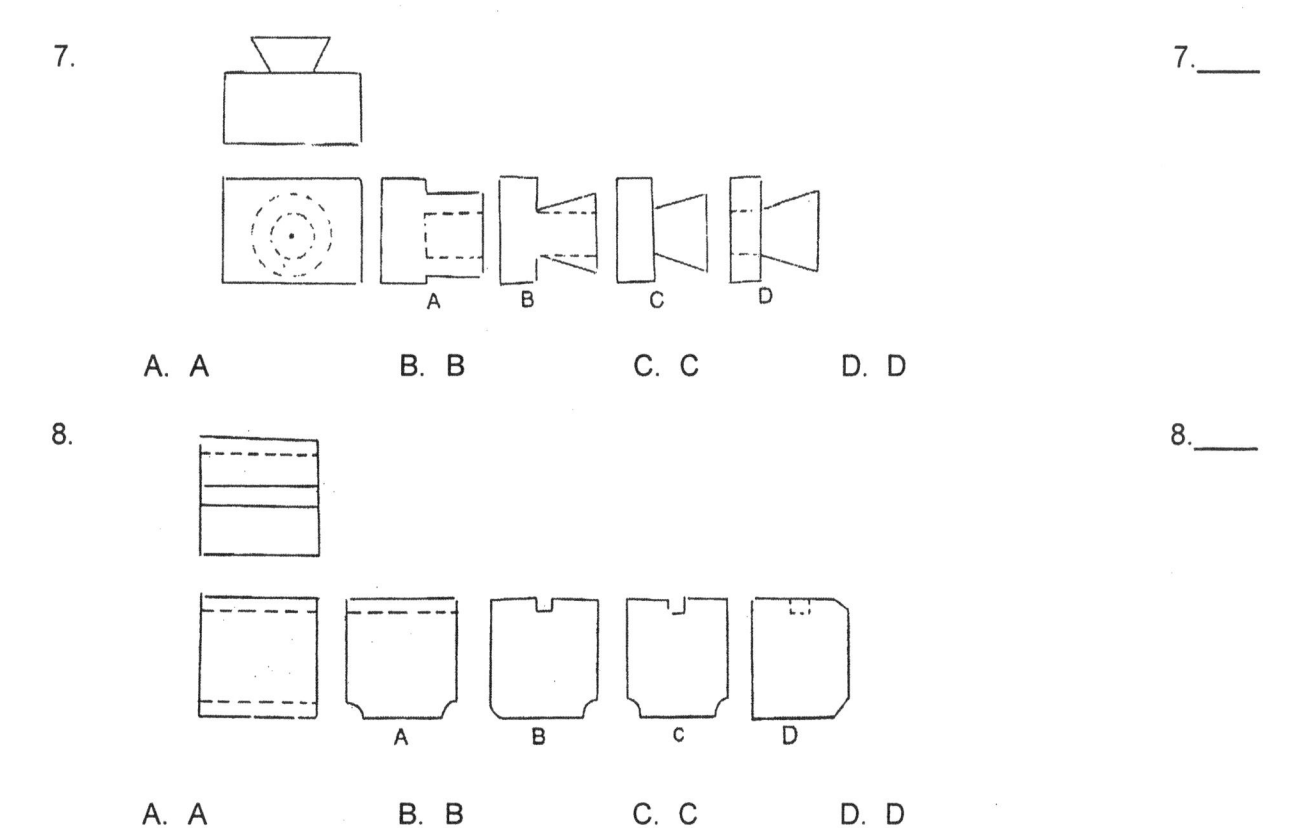

A. A B. B C. C D. D

7.____

8.

A. A B. B C. C D. D

8.____

9.

A. A B. B C. C D. D

10.

A. A B. B C. C D. D

11.

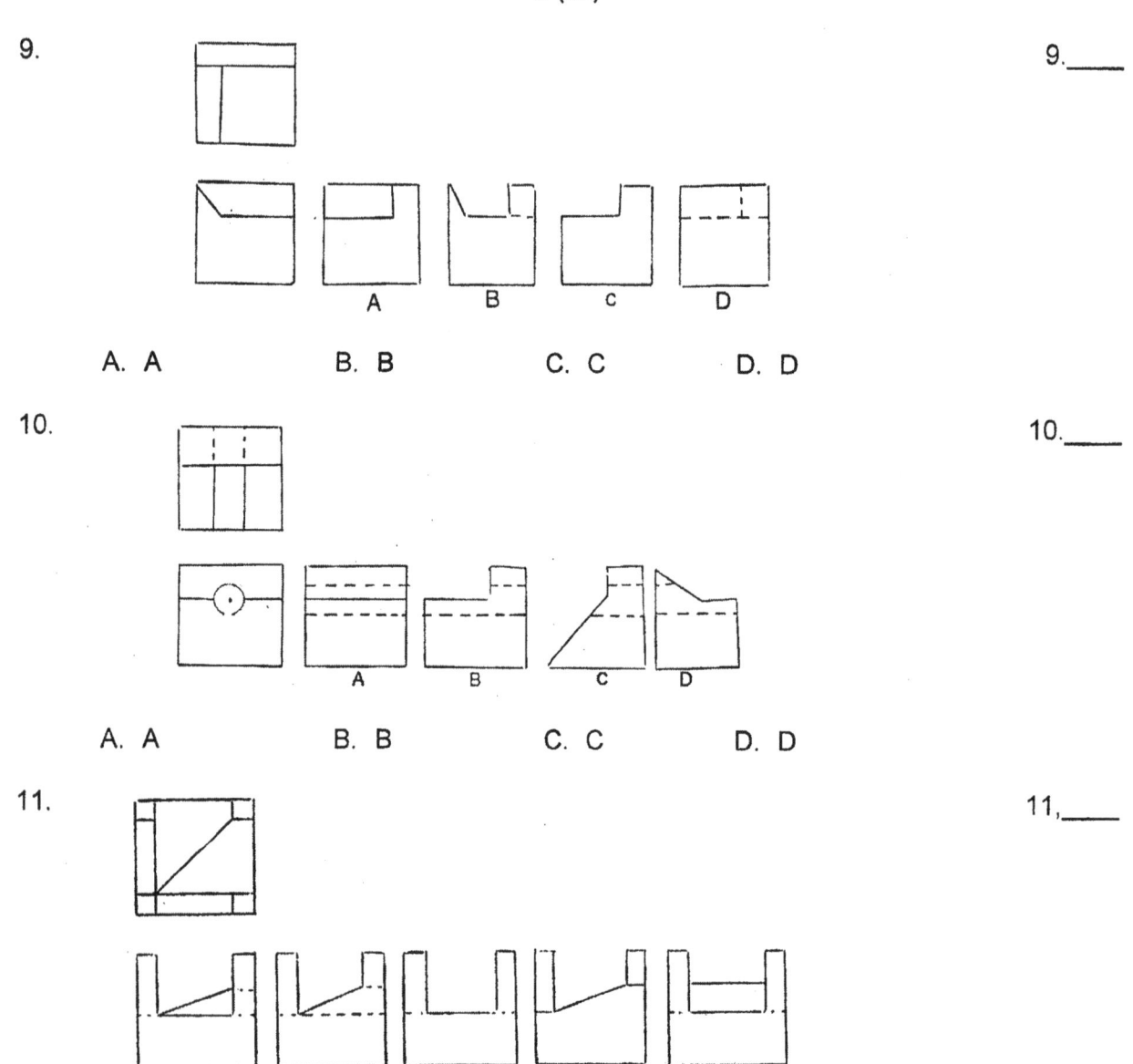

A. A B. B C. C D. D

Questions 12-14.

DIRECTIONS: Questions 12 through 14 are to be answered on the basis of the following sketch.

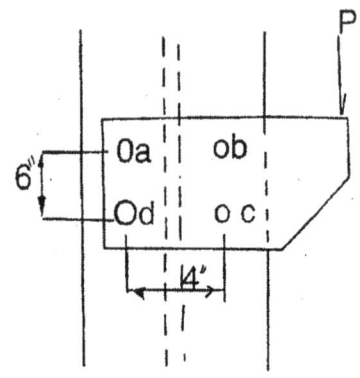

12. Maximum rivet stress occurs in rivet 12.____
    A. a only B. b only C. c only D. b and c

13. The plate carrying the load is known as a _____ plate. 13.____
    A. gusset B. flange C. web D. shear

14. The plate carrying the load is attached to a(n) _____ column. 14.____
    A. built-up B. H
    C. channel D. none of the above

15. A 3 x 3 x $^3/_8$ angle in a structural frame is in tension. It is connected at each 15.____
    end by one $^7/_8$" rivet to a gusset plate.
    The net section of the angle is equal to the gross minus _____ square inches.
    A. 0.339 B. 0.347 C. 0.375 D. 0.389

16. A formula commonly used to determine the allowable unit stresses in columns 16.____
    is s =
    A. $\dfrac{\pi^2 El}{4l^2}$
    B. $17000 - .485(\dfrac{1}{r})^2$
    C. $\dfrac{22500}{1+\dfrac{l^2}{1800r^2}}$
    D. $\dfrac{P+Mc}{A \pm I}$

17. A rectangular footing 6'0" long by 4'0" wide carries a vertical load of 20,000 17.____
    pounds located on the long axis 5 inches from the center of the footing.
    The maximum soil pressure under the footing due to this load is, in pounds per
    square inch, MOST NEARLY
    A. 1250 B. 1350 C. 1450 D. 1550

18. *Special anchorage* in concrete work commonly refers to 18.____
    A. reinforcement in concrete bolted to steel girders
    B. wing walls on a retaining wall to provide extra support
    C. a hook at the end of a reinforcing rod in continuous beam construction
    D. additional steel dowels connecting a concrete column with a concrete
       footing

Questions 19-20.

DIRECTIONS: Questions 19 and 20 are to be answered on the basis of the following sketch.

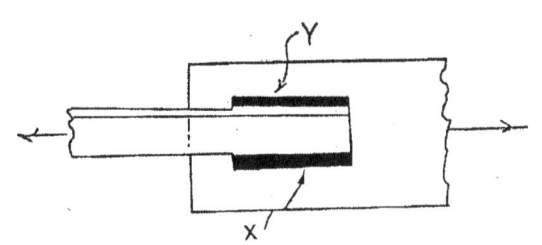

19. In the welded section shown, the length of weld x should be _____ that of y.   19.____
    A. equal to   B. greater than
    C. less than   D. independent of

20. The welds shown are _____ welds.   20.____
    A. single V   B. double V   C. plug   D. fillet

21. The slope at any point on the bending moment diagram for a beam is equal   21.____
    to the _____ the beam at that point.
    A. load on   B. shear on
    C. deflection of   D. slope of

22. The shear diagram for the beam shown in the   22.____
    diagram at the right is
    A. A
    B. B
    C. C
    D. D

23. Vertical curves in highway work are usually parts of   23.____
    A. circles   B. ellipses   C. hyperbolas   D. parabolas

24. In laying out an angle with a transit, an error of one minute will result in   24.____
    locating a point 1000 ft. from the transit off the true line by APPROXIMATELY
    _____ ft.
    A. 0.1   B. 0.2   C. 0.3   D. 0.5

25. The sum of the positive departures of a closed traverse exceeds that of the   25.____
    negative departures by 0.31 ft. The sum of the negative latitudes exceeds that
    of the positive latitudes by 0.67 ft.
    The linear error of closure is, in feet, MOST NEARLY
    A. 0.39   B. 0.47   C. 0.58   D. 0.74

26. The balanced latitudes and departures of the sides of a closed traverse are   26.____
    as follows:

Line	Lat.	Dep.
AB	+152.27	+212.06
BC	+316.19	+ 83.92
CD	-522.34	+119.30
DA	+ 53.88	-415.28

    The DMD of line CD referred to a meridian through A is
    A. 567.89   B. 635.46   C. 711.26   D. 819.77

Questions 27-31.

DIRECTIONS: Questions 27 through 31 are to be answered on the basis of the following closed traverse which is drawn to scale.

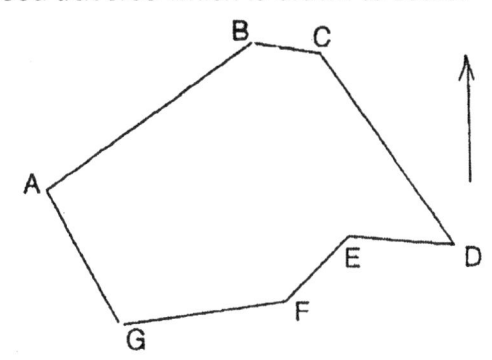

27. The sum of the interior angles of the traverse is 27.____
   A. 760°   B. 844°   C. 900°   D. 920°

28. The arithmetical sum of the deflection angles, i.e., the sum without regard to sign, is 28.____
   A. 160°
   B. 240°
   C. 330°
   D. greater than 360°

29. When balancing a survey of a closed traverse, the functions of angles most commonly used are 29.____
   A. sin and tan   B. cos and tan   C. sin and cos   D. tan and cot

30. Of the following lines, the one with the LARGEST departure is 30.____
   A. AB   B. CD   C. AG   D. GF

31. The area of the traverse could not be computed if all sides and angles were measured EXCEPT 31.____
   A. angles A, B, and C
   B. sides AB and CD and angle B
   C. side AB and angles A and B
   D. sides AB, BC, and CD

32. The notes for a level run are as follows: 32.____

Sta.	BS	HI	FS	Elev.
BM1	3.26			100.23
A	2.13		1.19	
B	4.05		3.20	
C	2.26		4.03	
BM2			4.22	

   The elevation of BMS is
   A. 99.17   B. 99.21   C. 99.25   D. 99.29

7 (#2)

33. The foot of a leveling rod has been worn through hard use so that the rod is now .02 ft. short.
The elevation of any point found, using this rod, will be
   A. .02 ft. low   B. correct   C. .02 ft. high   D. .04 ft. high

33.____

34. The correction to be applied to high rod readings on a Philadelphia rod is -0.004. In running a level circuit with this rod,
   A. 0.004 should be subtracted from all high rod readings before entering them
   B. the error should be ignored as it will cancel itself
   C. the error should be ignored until all elevations are computed and then corrections should be made to elevations as required
   D. the total error will be 0.004 times the square root of the number of high rod readings

34.____

Questions 35-40.

DIRECTIONS: Questions 35 through 40 are to be answered on the basis of the following sketch of a transit.

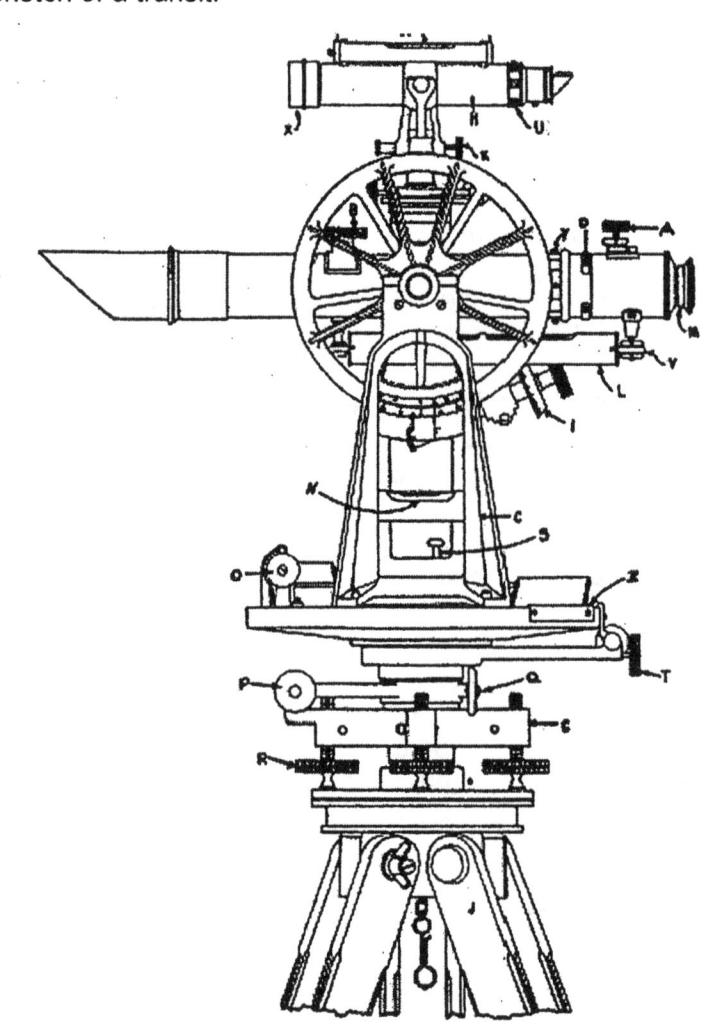

8 (#2)

35. The vertical circle is marked 35.____
    A. D   B. E   C. F   D. I

36. A prism would be attached at 36.____
    A. M   B. U   C. X   D. Z

37. The lower motion clamp is marked 37.____
    A. K   B. P   C. Q   D. T

38. The bubble which would normally be centered to make the line of sight truly horizontal is marked 38.____
    A. L   B. N   C. O   D. W

39. The needle lifting or needle release screw is marked 39.____
    A. D   B. K   C. R   D. S

40. A peg test for this transit has been performed, and the line of sight reads 4.085 on the far rod. The far rod reading is computed to be 4.060. In making the adjustment, the first thing to move is the 40.____
    A. bubble adjusting screws
    B. capstan-headed screws on the reticule
    C. vertical slow motion
    D. vertical Vernier adjusting screws

KEY (CORRECT ANSWERS)

1.	C	11.	A	21.	B	31.	D
2.	D	12.	D	22.	D	32.	D
3.	D	13.	A	23.	D	33.	B
4.	A	14.	B	24.	C	34.	C
5.	A	15.	C	25.	D	35.	C
6.	B	16.	B	26.	C	36.	A
7.	C	17.	A	27.	C	37.	C
8.	B	18.	C	28.	D	38.	A
9.	A	19.	C	29.	C	39.	D
10.	B	20.	D	30.	A	40.	C

SOLUTIONS TO PROBLEMS

3. **CORRECT ANSWER: D**
The tapes' lengths are based on a standardized tension. If extra tension is applied, a short reading will result.

4. **CORRECT ANSWER: A**
The correction to be applied is:
70/100 × .17 = 0.12
∴ 70.00 − 0.12 = 69.88

5. **CORRECT ANSWER: A**
200 ft. @ N45°E = 2 × 45 = 90°
300 ft. @ N60°E = $\frac{3}{5}$ × 60 = $\frac{180°}{270°}$

$AC = \frac{270°}{5} = N54°E$
$CA = S54°W$

6. **CORRECT ANSWER: B**
This is the definition of the stadia interval factor.

12. **CORRECT ANSWER: D**
The rivet stress is derived from the vertical load and the moment derived thereof. In this case, the vertical load is equal and the stresses due to moment are equal and additive to the vertical load. The moment stress is subtractive from the stresses on a and d.

15. **CORRECT ANSWER: C**
The net section = the gross minus the area taken by the rivet 1/8" larger than the rivet used.

The area subtracted = (8/8+1/8) × 3/8 = 0.375 in².

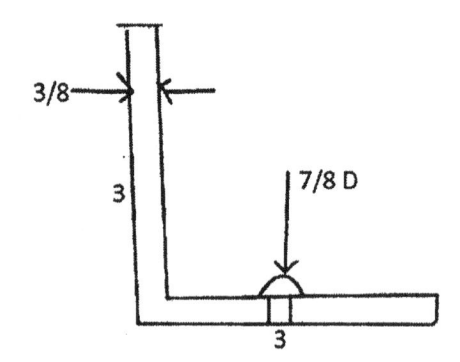

17. **CORRECT ANSWER: A**
Max. stress = $P/A + \frac{MC}{I}$ C = 3
$I = bh^3/12$

$= \frac{20}{6 \times 4} + \frac{(20 \times \frac{1}{2})(3)}{\frac{4 \times 6^3}{12}}$

$= \frac{20}{24} + \frac{15}{36} = .83 + .42 = 1.25$ K psf = 1250 psf

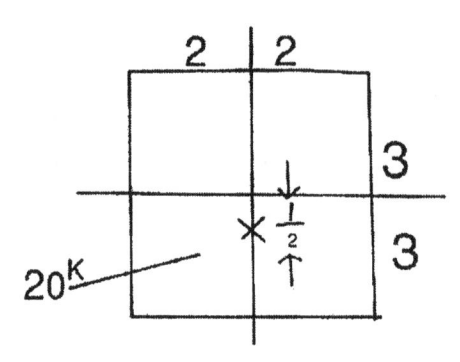

23. **CORRECT ANSWER: D**
Parabolic arc is ideally suited for changes in vertical grade since slope varies at constant rate with respect to horizontal distance.

24. **CORRECT ANSWER: C**
tan 1 minute = 0.00029

α = 1 minute
b = 1000 ft.
$\frac{a}{b}$ = tanα

a = tanα × b = .00029 × 1000 ft. = 0.29 ft.

25. **CORRECT ANSWER: D**

Linear error of closure $= \sqrt{(\sum Lat)^2 + (\sum Dep)^2}$

$= \sqrt{(0.31)^2 + (.67)^2}$

$= \sqrt{5450}$

$= 0.74$ ft.

26. **CORRECT ANSWER: C**
AB DMD = 212.06
BC DMD = 212.06 + 212.06 + 83.92 = 508.04
CD DMD = 508.04 + 83.92 + 119.30 = 711.26

The DMD of the first line equals the departure of the first line. The DMD of any other line is equal to the DMD of the preceding line plus the departure of the preceding line, plus the departure of the line itself.

27. **CORRECT ANSWER: C**
(n-2) × 180° = sum of the interior angles
n = number of sides
(7-2) × 180 = 900°

31. **CORRECT ANSWER: D**
There is no way to determine the lengths of these sides. All other missing data could be computed by trigonometry and geometry.

32. CORRECT ANSWER: D
The complete notes should read as follows:

Sta.	BS	HI	FS	Elev.
BM1	3.26	103.49		100.23
A	2.13	104.43	1.19	102.30
B	4.05	105.28	3.20	101.23
C	2.26	103.51	4.03	101.25
BM2			4.22	99.29

33. CORRECT ANSWER: B
Elevations are determined by differences of rod readings; therefore, a short rod does not affect the final data.

TEST 3

DIRECTIONS: Each question or incomplete statement is followed by several suggested answers or completions. Select the one that BEST answers the question or completes the statement. *PRINT THE LETTER OF THE CORRECT ANSWER IN THE SPACE AT THE RIGHT.*

1. A wooden beam is a rectangle 6" x 12". On a simple span, the ratio of the uniform load it can carry with the 6" sides vertical to that with the 12" sides vertical is as one is to
   A. 2   B. 5   C. 7   D. 9

2. A moving load consists of a 4-kip and an 8-kip concentrated load spaced 8 feet apart. The maximum bending moment caused by this moving load on a simple span of 16 feet is, in kip-feet,
   A. 33.3   B. 31.9   C. 27.6   D. 23.9

3. A canal with a trapezoidal cross-section is 6'0" wide at the bottom and has side slopes of one on one. When the depth of water is 4'6", the hydraulic radius is
   A. 2.43   B. 2.52   C. 2.55   D. 2.67

4. The minimum amount of cover required for water mains in city streets is NOT affected by
   A. depth of frost
   B. consideration of shock loads
   C. depth of rock
   D. any of the above

5. A vertical steel tank, 10'0" diameter, wall thickness ¼", is subjected to a hydrostatic pressure of 100 feet of water. The maximum tensile stress in the tank, in lb./sq.in., is MOST NEARLY
   A. 10,200   B. 10,400   C. 10,600   D. 10,800

6. Three eye bars, 6" x 1" x 25'0", jointly, are to carry a load of 200,000 lbs. The middle bar is .03 inch too short. Assuming the pins through the eyes to be parallel, the cross-section of the bars to be uniform throughout their entire length, and $E = 30 \times 10^6$ #/sq.in., the stress in the outer bars in lb./sq.in. will be MOST NEARLY
   A. 10,100   B. 10,300   C. 10,500   D. 10,800

7. A property of steel NOT usually determined in the ordinary commercial tensile test of steel is
   A. modulus of rupture
   B. percent reduction in area
   C. yield point
   D. ultimate stress

8. In the activated sludge process, *seeding* is carried on in the
   A. grit chamber
   B. aeration tank
   C. sand filter
   D. sedimentation tank

9. The hydraulic radius is defined as
   A. the distance from the center of gravity of cross-sectional area of flow to the point of minimum velocity
   B. the cross-sectional area of waterway divided by the wetted perimeter
   C. half the depth of flow
   D. the depth from the free surface to the point of maximum velocity

10. Water flowing from an orifice in the side of a tank strikes the ground at a point 10 feet, below the orifice and 5 feet from the tank.
    If the coefficient of velocity is 1.00, the height of water above the orifice, in feet, is MOST NEARLY
    A. .63   B. 1.73   C. 3.5   D. 7.9

11. Of the following formulas, the one that is MOST commonly used in determining the runoff from a watershed is Q =
    A. $A\frac{1.486}{M}R^{2/3}S^{1/2}$ B. Aci C. $CLH^{3/2}$ D. $AC\sqrt{RS}$

12. Maximum discharge in a circular sewer occurs when the ratio of the depth of flow to the diameter of the pipe is MOST NEARLY
    A. .5   B. .6   C. .9   D. 1.1

13. Of the following items, the one that is LEAST important in the design of a concrete pier is
    A. corrosion   B. erosion   C. scour   D. elutriation

14. Of the following items, the one which is LEAST related to the others is
    A. extensometer   B. weir
    C. piezometer   D. hook gauge

15. In a through truss bridge, a horizontal longitudinal member acting as a beam to support loads is known as a
    A. floor beam   B. portal brace
    C. lower chord   D. stringer

16. Using pipe A alone, a given tank is filled with water in 5 minutes. When pipe B is used alone, the same tank is filled in 7 minutes.
    If both pipes are used at the same time, the length of time required to fill this tank is, in minutes, MOST NEARLY
    A. 2.87   B. 2.92   C. 2.99   D. 3.05

17. In plane surveying, double meridian distances are used to compute the _____ of a traverse.
    A. latitudes and departures
    B. area
    C. error of closure
    D. corrections for magnetic declination for the sides

3 (#3)

18. The deflection angle required to lay out a 50 ft. chord of a 3°00' circular curve is MOST NEARLY
    A. 0°45'   B. 1°45'   C. 2°30'   D. 3°45'

19. Of the following, the one that is NOT a method of locating details for topography is
    A. offset distance
    B. range line
    C. tie line
    D. string line

20. *Blocking in* is a practice followed when it is necessary to
    A. set up a transit on line between two stations
    B. prolong a line around an obstacle
    C. project a high point to the ground
    D. set a point on line by double centering

21. Of the following terms, the one that is LEAST related to the others is
    A. five level section
    B. slope stake
    C. mass diagram
    D. hydraulic fill

22. Using a given 100 foot tape, the slope distance between two points on a 2% grade is found to be 250.26. When checked later, the tape is found to be 100.02 ft. long.
    The horizontal distance between the two points is MOST NEARLY
    A. 250.21   B. 250.26   C. 250.29   D. 250.32

23. When it is impossible to balance the foresight and backsight distances, precise difference in elevations may be obtained by _____ leveling.
    A. trigonometric
    B. reciprocal
    C. stadia
    D. barometric

24. Specifications usually require that controlled concrete develop its design strength
    A. when forms are stripped
    B. in 28 days
    C. in 7 days
    D. in 2 months

25. Horizontal reinforcing in the exposed face of a cantilever retaining wall is necessary PRIMARILY to reinforce against _____ stress.
    A. tensile
    B. compressive
    C. shearing
    D. shrinkage

KEY (CORRECT ANSWERS)

1.	A		11.	B
2.	A		12.	C
3.	B		13.	D
4.	C		14.	A
5.	B		15.	D
6.	A		16.	B
7.	A		17.	B
8.	B		18.	A
9.	B		19.	D
10.	A		20.	A

21. D
22. B
23. B
24. C
25. D

EXAMINATION SECTION
TEST 1

DIRECTIONS: Each question or incomplete statement is followed by several suggested answers or completions. Select the one that BEST answers the question or completes the statement. *PRINT THE LETTER OF THE CORRECT ANSWER IN THE SPACE AT THE RIGHT.*

1. Dowels connecting adjacent roadway slabs are used primarily to

    A. transmit compressive stress to adjacent slabs
    B. reinforce against temperature stress
    C. reinforce against shrinkage stress
    D. prevent differential settlement of slabs

2. Good practice requires that the minimum overhead clearance at the crown for an underpass at the intersection of two highways be MOST NEARLY _____ feet.

    A. 10   B. 14   C. 17   D. 19

3. A simple beam on an 18'0" span carries a uniformly distributed load including its own weight of 200 pounds per foot.
   If a jack is placed under the midspan and the midpoint jacked up so it is at the same elevation as the ends, the load on the jack, in pounds, will be

    A. 960
    C. 1800
    B. 1600
    D. more than 1800

4. Of the following, the one which is NOT the symbol for a standard beam connection is

    A. A3   B. B3   C. H3   D. T3

5. Of the following items, the one that is NOT important in determining the minimum length of vertical curve required to connect two intersecting grades is

    A. maximum speed of vehicle
    B. grades of tangents
    C. whether intersection is at a summit or a sag
    D. crown of road

6. For an angle of intersection of 16°30', tables of the functions of a one-degree curve show the middle ordinate to be 59.30 feet.
   For the same angle of intersection, the middle ordinate for a curve whose radius is 1433 feet is MOST NEARLY

    A. 14.83   B. 24.94   C. 67.35   D. 183.72

7. The *Proctor Test* is used in testing

    A. asphalt   B. concrete   C. soils   D. mortar

8. Within the cross-section of a WF beam, the horizontal shearing stress is a maximum at the

A. midpoint of the beam
B. outermost fiber of the compression flange
C. outermost fiber of the tension flange
D. point of intersection of web and flange

9. The maximum load allowed on a 3/8" fillet weld, 6" long, when the allowable shearing stress is 13,000 #/sq.in. is MOST NEARLY, in pounds,

   A. 20,700   B. 21,900   C. 24,300   D. 26,370

10. A closed level circuit was run starting at BM A. The elevation of A on closing the circuit was found to be 0.097 lower than at the start.
    Of the following, the MOST logical reason for this error, barring mistakes, is the

    A. length of the rod was not standard due either to a uniform expansion or contraction
    B. level settled after the backsights had been read
    C. turning points settled after the foresights had been read
    D. line of sight was inclined upward and each foresight distance exceeded the corresponding backsight distance

11. The sensitivity of the bubble tube of an engineer's level can best be measured by

    A. measuring the distance between etched lines on the vial
    B. taking readings on a rod a known distance away with bubble in two different positions
    C. making a two-peg test
    D. measuring the curvature of the etched surface of the vial

12. Of the following, the MOST important source of accidental error in ordinary leveling work is

    A. change in length of leveling rod due to change in temperature
    B. axis of level tube not perpendicular to vertical axis
    C. eye piece is not focused accurately
    D. failure to wave rod

13. When taking a single measure of the horizontal angle between two points which differ greatly in elevation, the MOST important of the following relationships in the transit is

    A. axis of long bubble parallel to line of sight
    B. transverse axis perpendicular to vertical axis
    C. index correction of vertical arc equal to zero
    D. vertical cross-hair in plane perpendicular to transverse axis

14. Of the following factors, the one that is LEAST important in determining the total amount of superelevation required at the edge of pavement on a horizontal curve is

    A. speed of vehicle   B. weight of vehicle
    C. radius of curve   D. width of pavement

15. If the horizontal circle of a transit is graduated to 20' and 39 divisions on the limb equal 40 civisions on the vernier, then the LEAST count of the vernier is

    A. 14"   B. 28"   C. 30"   D. 1'6"

16. The slump test for concrete is used to determine the   16.____

    A. strength   B. consistency
    C. water ratio   D. segregation

17. The following notes are taken from the survey of a closed traverse with five sides: 17.____

at	Deflection Angles
A	R 65° 25'
B	L 45° 14'
C	R 135° 42'
D	R 92° 17'
E	

    The value of the deflection angle at E is MOST NEARLY
    A. 111°22'   B. 111°34'   C. 111°46'   D. 111°50'

18. A Williot-Mohr diagram is used to determine   18.____

    A. deflection in trusses
    B. wind stress in framed bents
    C. diagonal shear in beams
    D. uplift pressure on the base of a cam

19. A reinforced concrete beam is 10" wide by 16" effective depth. If fs = 20,000 lb./sq.in., fc = 1350 lb./sq.in. and n = 10, then the value of k is MOST NEARLY   19.____

    A. .367   B. .373   C. .403   D. .419

20. Of the following concrete structures, the one in which gunite is MOST likely to be used is   20.____

    A. footings   B. piles   C. walls   D. beams

21. For soil sampling in hardpan, the BEST method to use is   21.____

    A. jet probing   B. wash boring
    C. auger boring   D. core boring

22. The bending moment at the ends of a beam fully restrained at both ends which supports a uniform load of w pounds per foot throughout its entire length l is   22.____

    A. $\frac{wl^2}{8}$ B. $\frac{wl}{10}$ C. $\frac{wl^2}{10}$ D. $\frac{wl^2}{12}$

23. A reinforced concrete beam 10" wide by 16" effective depth is subjected to an end shear of 15,000 lbs.   23.____
    If fs = 20,000 #/sq.in., fc = 2500 #/sq.in., u = 187 #/sq.in., and j = .857, the perimeter of steel required to reinforce against the shear, in inches, is MOST NEARLY

    A. 2.38   B. 3.72   C. 5.85   D. 6.94

24. A precast reinforced concrete beam 20'0" long, weight 50 #/ft. is to be lifted by two slings symmetrically placed.   24.____
    For minimum bending stress in the beam, the distance from an end to a point of support, in feet, is MOST NEARLY

A. 3.98   B. 4.15   C. 4.35   D. 5.15

25. For maximum stress in *ab*, the distance the load *P* should be from the wall is MOST NEARLY
    A. 10'7"
    B. 11'9"
    C. 13'3"
    D. 15'0"

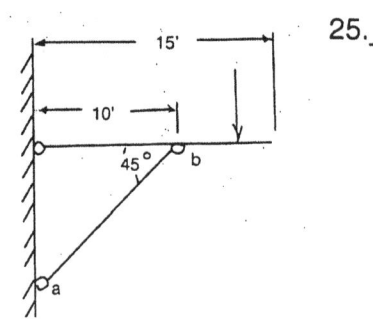

25. ____

KEY (CORRECT ANSWERS)

1.	D	11.	B
2.	B	12.	C
3.	D	13.	B
4.	D	14.	B
5.	D	15.	C
6.	A	16.	B
7.	C	17.	D
8.	A	18.	A
9.	A	19.	C
10.	D	20.	C

21. D
22. D
23. C
24. B
25. D

TEST 2

DIRECTIONS: Each question or incomplete statement is followed by several suggested answers or completions. Select the one that BEST answers the question or completes the statement. *PRINT THE LETTER OF THE CORRECT ANSWER IN THE SPACE AT THE RIGHT.*

1. The rod reading at Sta. 100+27 is 4.26. With the same H.I., the rod reading at Sta. 103+16 is 6.34.
   The grade between the two stations is MOST NEARLY

   A. +0.72%   B. +0.79%   C. -0.72%   D. -0.79%

2. In taping a distance known to be 2000 ft. long, the distance is found to be 1900.02 ft. The error is MOST probably caused by

   A. neglecting temperature correction
   B. neglecting to record one tape length
   C. tension on tape not standard
   D. wind blowing tape out of line

3. The sum of the deflection angles for a closed traverse, where *n* equals the number of sides of the traverse, is

   A. (n-2)180°   B. 180°n   C. (n-l)360°   D. 360°

4. When a level rod is *waved,* the correct reading is the

   A. largest reading
   B. smallest reading
   C. average of the largest and the smallest reading
   D. difference between the largest and the smallest reading

5. A topographic map to a scale of 1:2400 has a 5-foot vertical interval. A straight line on the map connecting two adjacent contours is 0.437 inches long.
   The slope of this line is, in percent, MOST NEARLY

   A. 5.6   B. 5.7   C. 5.8   D. 6.0

6. A Philadelphia rod is fully extended and the distance from the 1-foot mark to the 11-foot mark is measured and found to be 10.005.
   In a level circuit, a high-rod reading on this rod is

   A. 0.005 too large
   B. 0.005 too small
   C. considered correct since the errors will balance out
   D. correct if the rod is waved

7. A differential leveling circuit without sideshots was run between two bench marks. The level was set up x times.
   The number of turning points used was

   A. 2x   B. x-2   C. x-1   D. x

8. A closed traverse is usually preferred to an open traverse because

A. more ground can be covered
B. a mathematical check on the work is provided
C. the area can be determined
D. the computations are easier

9. The difference in elevation between two points on the hydraulic gradient of a pipe of uniform diameter is a measure of the loss of _____ head.

    A. potential   B. pressure   C. velocity   D. total

10. Of the following values of f in the formula $h = f \dfrac{l}{d} \dfrac{V^2}{2g}$, the one which would MOST probably apply to a smooth pipe is

    A. 0.02   B. 0.11   C. 0.31   D. 0.41

11. The required cross-sectional area of a culvert is a function of

    A. width of roadway   B. depth of fill
    C. drainage area served   D. headwall area

12. The value of k for a particular reinforced concrete beam is 0.400. The value of j for this beam is MOST NEARLY

    A. 0.873   B. 0.870   C. 0.867   D. 0.865

13. A steel bar one inch in diameter is imbedded a distance of 30 inches in a mass of concrete.
If the bar is subjected to axial pull of 10,000#, the bond stress is, in pounds per square inch, MOST NEARLY

    A. 106   B. 108   C. 112   D. 116

14. The slump test for concrete is a measure of

    A. water-cement ratio   B. consistency
    C. strength   D. size of aggregate

15. The term *special anchorage* in concrete construction refers to

    A. an anchor bolt to tie a beam to a wall
    B. tieing the reinforcement to a steel beam
    C. a U-shaped bar to take care of shearing stresses
    D. a hook at the end of a reinforcing bar

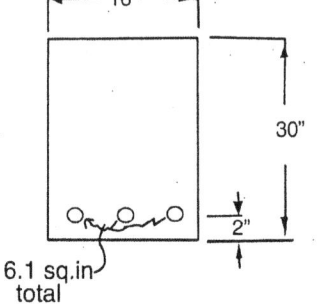

16.

16" wide, 30" tall, 2" cover, 6.1 sq.in total

$$k = \dfrac{1}{2} f_c k 2 j = 236$$

Assuming exactly balanced design, the maximum bending moment that can be carried by the reinforced concrete beam in the accompanying sketch is, in inch pounds, MOST NEARLY

   A. 2,960,000   B. 3,420,370   C. 4,160,500   D. 5,180,600

17. The maximum deflection of a simple beam on a span l carrying a uniformly distributed load of w per unit length is $\frac{5}{384}\frac{w}{EI}$ multiplied by

   A. l^2 B. l^3 C. l^4 D. l^7

18. The section modulus of a beam is

   A. $\int y^2 dA$ B. $\frac{V}{Ib}A\bar{y}$ C. $\frac{\sqrt{I}}{A}$ D. $\frac{I}{c}$

19. A timber beam 3" x 12" (actual dimensions) is simply supported on a clear span of 9'0" and carries a uniform load of 1000 #/ft. throughout its entire length.
The maximum bending stress in the beam is, in lbs./sq.in., MOST NEARLY

   A. 1570   B. 1690   C. 1745   D. 1860

20. A wooden beam 8 inches wide by 12 inches deep (actual dimensions) carries a uniform load of 600 pounds per foot including its own weight on a simple span of 16'0".
The MAXIMUM shear stress intensity in the beam is, in pounds per square inch,

   A. 70   B. 71   C. 72   D. 75

21. The horizontal component of the reaction at joint B in the accompanying diagram is MOST NEARLY

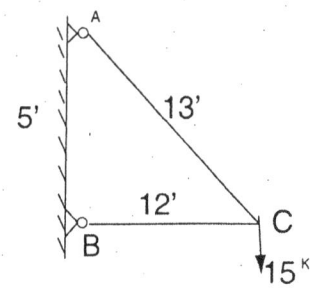

   A. 32K
   B. 36K
   C. 40K
   D. 44K

22. The yield point of a ductile metal is that unit stress at which

   A. the stress ceases to be proportional to the strain
   B. there is an increase in deformation with no increase in stress
   C. the material ruptures
   D. the metal ceases to act as an elastic material

Questions 23-27.

DIRECTIONS: Questions 23 through 27 refer to the sketch of the beam and girder connection shown below.

4 (#2)

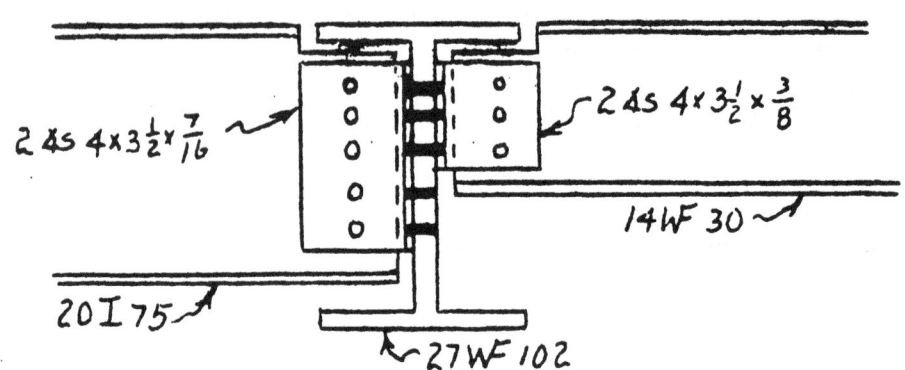

Diagram shows a steel connection with labels: 2 ∠s 4×3½×7/16, 2 ∠s 4×3½×3/8, 14WF30, 20I75, 27WF102.

23. The diameter of the rivets used would MOST likely be 23.____

    A. 5/8"   B. 7/8"   C. 1 3/16"   D. 1 5/8"

24. Of the following allowable stresses, the only one that would be used in determining the number of rivets connecting the angles to the 20 I 75 is the allowable stress in 24.____

    A. single shear   B. end bearing
    C. web shear   D. enclosed bearing

25. The allowable load on rivet A is determined by the allowable stress in 25.____

    A. double shear   B. single shear
    C. tension   D. torsion

26. Both beams shown are 26.____

    A. chased   B. blocked   C. squared   D. clipped

27. The number of field rivets required in the connection is 27.____

    A. 4   B. 6   C. 9   D. 10

28. The term *batter* in concrete work refers to 28.____

    A. bracing of forms
    B. slope of finished surface
    C. consistency of concrete
    D. pressure of wet concrete in forms

29. Of the following items, the one that is LEAST related to the others is 29.____

    A. B.O.D.   B. Imhoff tank
    C. effluent   D. liquid limit

30. A beam on a simple span of 16'0" carries a concentrated load of 20 kips 5'0" from the left support and a uniform load of 3 kips per foot over the entire span.
The distance from the left support to the point of maximum moment is, in feet, MOST NEARLY 30.____

    A. 5.92   B. 5.97   C. 6.02   D. 6.07

31. A beam has a trapezoidal cross-section which is symmetrical about a vertical axis. The top width is 4 inches, the bottom width 8 inches, and the depth 6 inches.
The distance from the bottom of the beam to the neutral axis is, in inches, 31.____

A. 2.83 B. 2.75 C. 2.67 D. 2.59

32. The ends of a steel bar 1 inch square are set in rigid walls spaced 4'0" in the clear. Another square steel bar 2 inches on a side is set in rigid walls spaced 8'0" in the clear. The ratio of the unit stress in the longer bar to that in the shorter bar due to an increase in temperature is

    A. 3/8 B. 5/8 C. 1 D. 3/2

32._____

Questions 33-35.

DIRECTIONS: Questions 33 through 35 refer to the truss shown below.

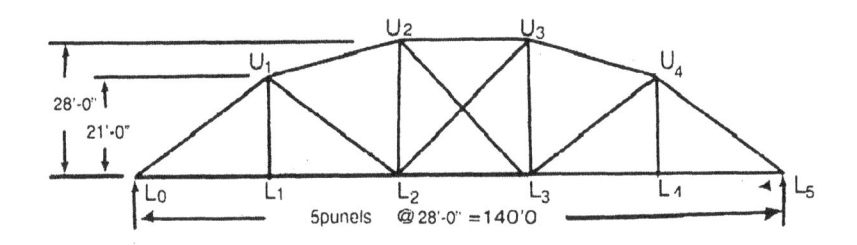

33. To obtain the stress in U_1L_2, the truss should be cut between U_1L_1 and U_2L_2 and moments taken about

    A. U_2
    B. L_1
    C. L_0
    D. a point to the left of L_0

33._____

34. The stress in member L_1L_2 for a load of one kip per foot extending over the entire span is, in kips, MOST NEARLY

    A. 74.67 B. 75.33 C. 75.67 D. 76.00

34._____

35. The stress in member U_2U_3 for a load of one kip per foot extending over the entire span is, in kips, MOST NEARLY

    A. 83.15 B. 83.30 C. 83.45 D. 84.00

35._____

36. In taping a distance on a 6% slope, the slope distance was measured.
    The correction per hundred feet to be applied to the measured distance is, in feet,

    A. 0.09 B. 0.12 C. 0.15 D. 0.18

36._____

37. The linear error of closure of a traverse is computed to be 0.04 feet. The sum of the lengths of the sides is 793.26 ft.
    The precision of the survey should be recorded as

    A. $\dfrac{0.04}{600}$ B. $\dfrac{4}{79326}$ C. $\dfrac{4}{793.26}$ D. $\dfrac{1}{19800}$

37._____

38. Errors due to eccentricity in the plates of a transit can be eliminated by   38.____
   A. reading the angle twice, once with the telescope normal, the second time with the telescope inverted
   B. using the averaged reading of the A and B verniers
   C. accurate leveling of the transit
   D. using two observers

39. A transit is set up at Sta. B and the deflection angle to Sta. C is measured (backsight on Sta. A) and found to be 22°15' R.   39.____
   The value of the angle ABC, measured clockwise from A to C, is

   A. 69°30'   B. 108°45'   C. 144°15'   D. 202°15'

40. The elevations of the P.V.C., P.V.I., and P.V.T. of a symmetrical vertical curve are 100.26, 103.26, and 98.76, respectively.   40.____
   The elevation of the midpoint of the vertical curve is MOST NEARLY

   A. 98.63   B. 99.72   C. 101.38   D. 103.17

KEY (CORRECT ANSWERS)

1.	C	11.	C	21.	B	31.	C
2.	B	12.	C	22.	B	32.	C
3.	D	13.	A	23.	B	33.	D
4.	B	14.	B	24.	D	34.	A
5.	B	15.	D	25.	B	35.	D
6.	A	16.	A	26.	B	36.	D
7.	C	17.	C	27.	D	37.	D
8.	B	18.	D	28.	B	38.	B
9.	D	19.	B	29.	D	39.	D
10.	A	20.	D	30.	A	40.	C

TEST 3

DIRECTIONS: Each question or incomplete statement is followed by several suggested answers or completions. Select the one that BEST answers the question or completes the statement. *PRINT THE LETTER OF THE CORRECT ANSWER IN THE SPACE AT THE RIGHT.*

1. In highway work, the degree of curve is commonly defined as the angle

   A. at the center subtended by an arc 100 ft. in length
   B. at the center subtending the entire curve
   C. at which the two tangents to the curve intersect
   D. between a tangent and a chord 100 ft. in length

2. The term *magnetic declination* refers to the

   A. attraction on a magnetic needle of nearby metallic objects
   B. dip of a magnetic needle
   C. angle between a given line and the meridian
   D. angle between true north and magnetic north

3. The bearings of the sides of a closed quadrilateral are:

   AB - N12°15'W
   BC - N15°10'E
   CD - S60°20'E
   DA - S18°30'W

   The interior angle CDA of the quadrilateral is

   A. 87°25'   B. 10°110'   C. 126°40'   D. 154°15'

4. In a given triangle, side a = 220 ft. and the angle opposite is 30°00'.
   If angle B = 45°00', then the side opposite angle B, in feet, is MOST NEARLY

   A. 311   B. 327   C. 346   D. 411

5. Of the following statements, the one that is CORRECT is:

   A. Blue ink is used when making tracings for blueprint work
   B. If ink lines on a tracing do not dry quickly, they should be blotted
   C. Vertical dimensions should be lettered so that they read from the right side of the sheet
   D. Dimension lines should be of the same weight as lines used in the views

6. A common method of lengthening the life of a wooden pile is by impregnating it with

   A. white lead   B. red lead
   C. sodium silicate   D. creosote

7. The MOST common unit for measuring excavation is

   A. cubic yard   B. cubic foot
   C. ton   D. pound

8. The width of each lane in a modern two-lane highway would MOST likely be 8.____

   A. 8'   B. 12'   C. 16'   D. 20'

Questions 9-11.

DIRECTIONS: Questions 9 through 11 refer to the figure shown below. (Any trigonomatic computation required is to be done by slide rule.)

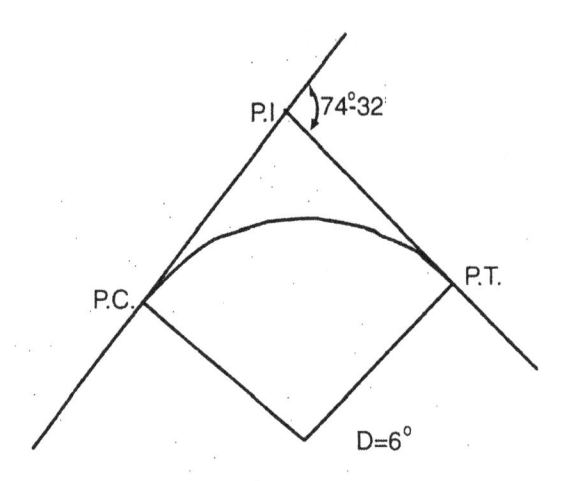

9. The station of the P.C. is 17+57.2. 9.____
   The deflection angle from the P.C. to Sta. 19 is MOST NEARLY

   A. 2°39'   B. 3°17'   C. 4°17'   D. 6°17'

10. The radius of the curve is, in feet, MOST NEARLY 10.____

    A. 955   B. 960   C. 970   D. 980

11. The station of the P.T. is MOST NEARLY 11.____

    A. 29+99.2   B. 29+99.4   C. 29+99.6   D. 30+00.4

12. Two cylindrical tanks with vertical axes lie one above the other. The lower tank is 8'0" in diameter and 8'0" high. The upper tank is 4'0" in diameter and 40'0" high with its base at the level of the top of the lower tank. The lower tank is full of water, and the upper tank is empty. 12.____
    The energy, in foot-pounds, required to pump the water from the lower to the upper tank is MOST NEARLY

    A. 502,000   B. 505,000   C. 508,000   D. 511,000

Questions 13-18.

DIRECTIONS: Questions 13 through 18 refer to the sketch of the plate girder shown below.

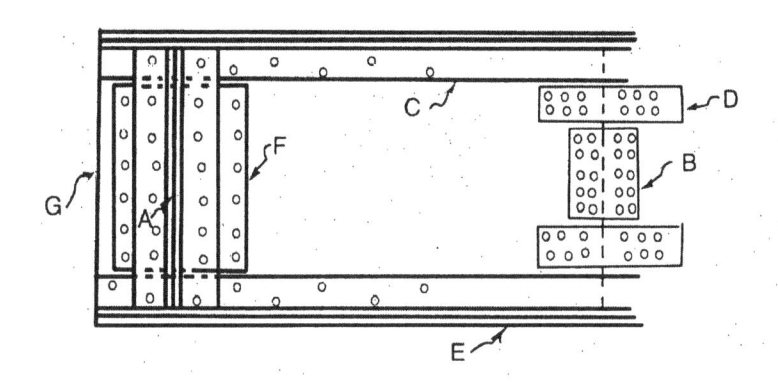

For each of the parts of the plate girder listed below in Questions 13 through 18, select the letter representing that part in the sketch above. For each of questions 13 through 18, the correct answer is

A. A   B. B   C. C   D. D   E. E   F. F   G. G

13. Flange angle   13._____

14. Shear splice   14._____

15. Stiffener   15._____

16. Cover plate   16._____

17. Web   17._____

18. Filler plate   18._____

19. Of the following symbols, the one that represents the ratio of the modulus of elasticity of steel to the modulus of elasticity of concrete in concrete design is   19._____

     A. k   B. v   C. p   D. n

20. A rectangular gate 4'0" wide by 6'0" high is submerged in water with the 4'0" side parallel to and 2'0" below the water surface. The gate is in a vertical plane.
The total pressure on the gate is, in pounds, MOST NEARLY   20._____

     A. 7480   B. 7590   C. 7660   D. 7720

21. The distance from the top of the gate to the center of pressure of the water on one side of the gate described in the preceding question is, in feet, MOST NEARLY   21._____

     A. 3.60   B. 3.70   C. 3.80   D. 3.90

22. Reservoir A is connected to Reservoir B by two parallel pipes, one 6 inches in diameter, the other 12 inches in diameter. The friction factor, f, is the same for each pipe.
If the flow in the 12-inch pipe is 6 cubic feet per second, the flow in the 6-inch pipe is, in cubic feet per second, MOST NEARLY   22._____

     A. 1.01   B. 1.03   C. 1.05   D. 1.06

23. The hydraulic radius of a rectangular channel 6'0" wide with a 4'0" depth of water is, in feet, MOST NEARLY   23._____

| A. 1.71 | B. 1.75 | C. 1.79 | D. 1.83 |

24. On a transit, the tangent screw is used to

    A. clamp the telescope in either erect or inverted position
    B. adjust the level bubbles
    C. focus the objective lens
    D. rotate the telescope small distances

25. The tangent of angle A is equal to

    A. $\sqrt{1-\cos^2 A}$ B. $\dfrac{\sec A}{\cos A}$ C. $\sin A \cos A$ D. $\dfrac{\sin A}{\cos A}$

26. If two stations on a mass diagram for earthwork have equal ordinates, the

    A. elevations of the two stations are the same
    B. end areas at the two stations are equal
    C. volume of cut equals the volume of fill between the two stations
    D. volume of fill between the two stations may be moved with equal economy to either station

27. The primary cause of parallax in a telescope is

    A. atmospheric disturbances
    B. maladjustment of the cross hairs
    C. improper focusing of the objective
    D. improper focusing of the eyepiece

28. The notes for a three level section for a roadway 20 ft. wide are as follows:

    $$\dfrac{c12}{16} \qquad \dfrac{c13}{0} \qquad \dfrac{c16}{18}$$

    The side slopes of the embankment are _____ horizontal to _____ vertical.
    A. 1; 2   B. 1; 1   C. 2; 1   D. 2; 3

29. Various combinations of the known parts of a triangle are given below. The combination which does NOT describe a unique triangle (i.e., one triangle and one only) is

    A. three sides
    B. two sides and the included angle
    C. one side and two angles
    D. two sides and an acute angle opposite one of the sides

30. To permit easier operation of vehicles, a tangent is MOST frequently connected to a horizontal circular curve by means of a

    A. reversed curve   B. spiral
    C. parabola   D. hyperbola

31. An alidade is MOST commonly used in conjunction with a

    A. transit   B. plane table
    C. barometer   D. tide gauge

32. The increase in length of a 100-foot stool tape due to a temperature rise of 15°F is, in feet, MOST NEARLY

   A. 0.0001   B. 0.0005   C. 0.01   D. 0.05

33. An instrument used to measure the area of a closed traverse, plotted to scale, is a

   A. integraph
   B. clinometer
   C. planimeter
   D. pantograph

Questions 34-35.

DIRECTIONS: Questions 34 and 35 refer to the following diagrams on the following page.

(Diagram for question 34.)   (Diagram for question 35.)

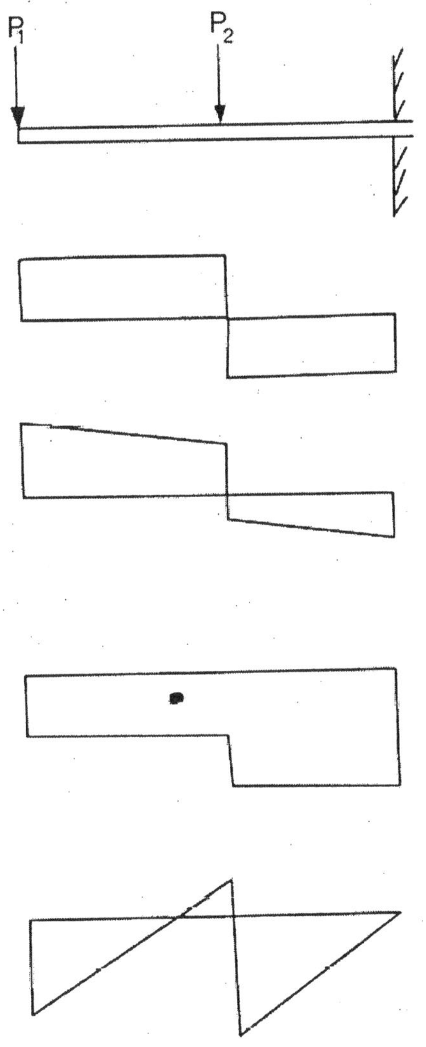

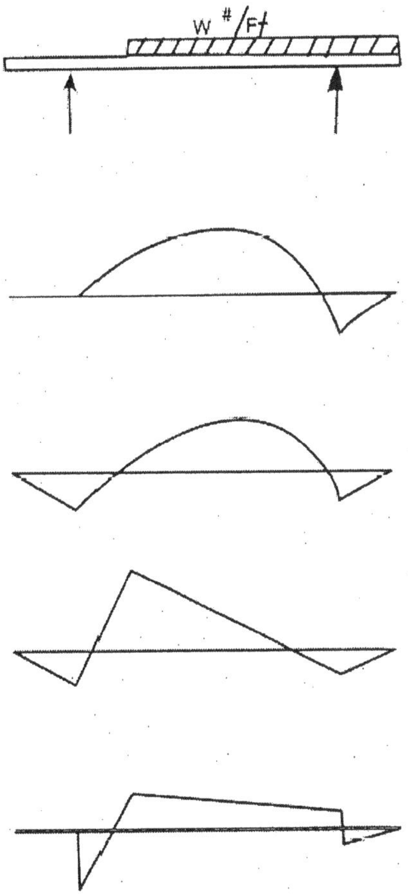

34. The shear diagram for the beam shown in the above diagram is (neglecting the weight of the beam)

   A. A   B. B   C. C   D. D

6 (#3)

35. The moment diagram for the beam shown in the above diagram is (neglecting the weight of the beam)   35._____

   A. A   B. B   C. C   D. D

Questions 36-40.

DIRECTIONS: In Questions 36 through 40, the plan and front elevation of an object are shown on the left, and on the right are shown four figures, one of which, and only one, represents the right side elevation. Print in the space at the right the letter which represents the right side elevation. In the sample shown below, which figure correctly represents the right side elevation?

   A. A   B. B   C. C   D. D

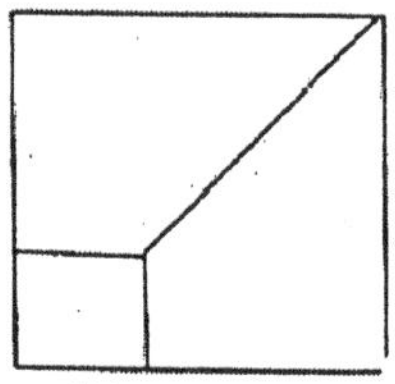

Plan

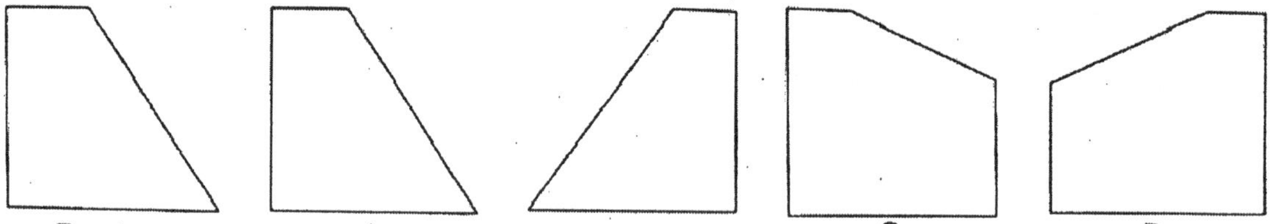

Front Elevation   A   B   C   D

The correct answer is A.

In Questions 36 through 40, which figure correctly represents the right side elevation?
   A. A   B. B   C. C   D. D

36.   36._____

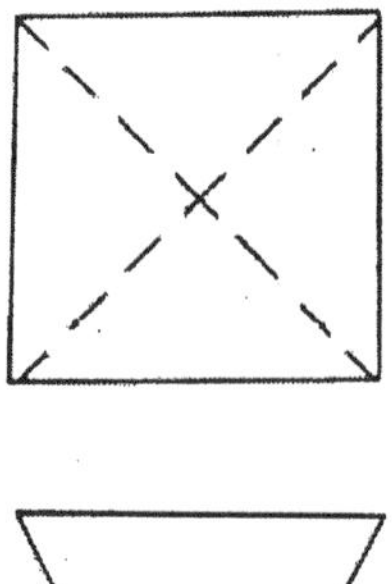

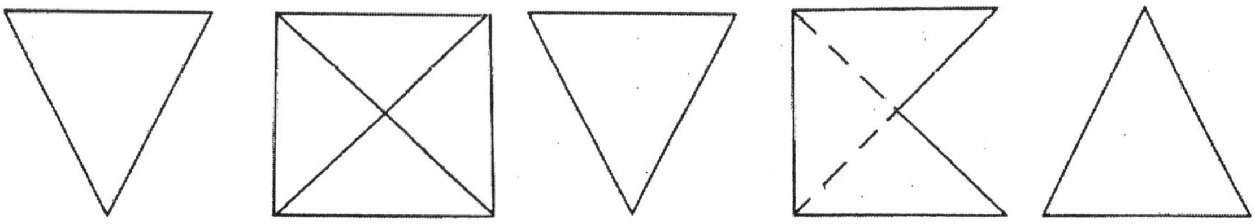

A   B   C   D

37. Questions 37-40.   37. _____

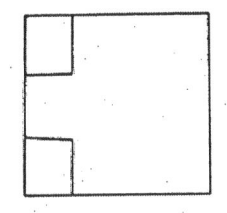

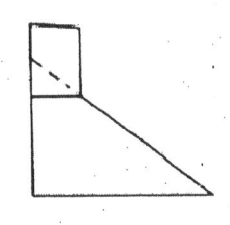

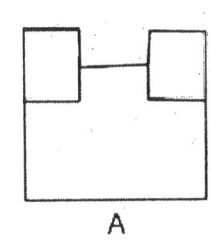

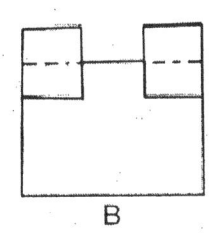

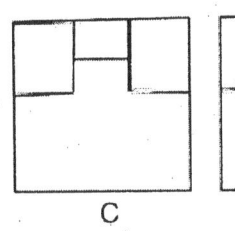

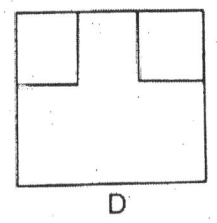

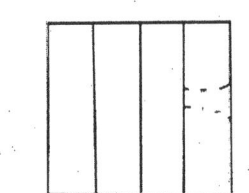

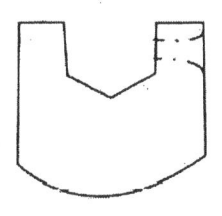

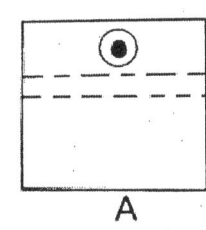

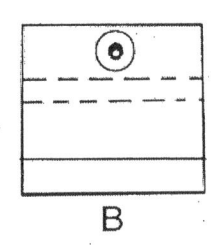

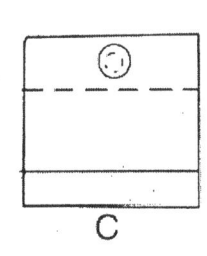

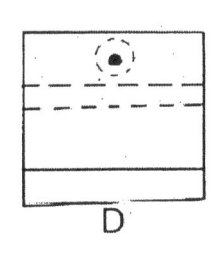

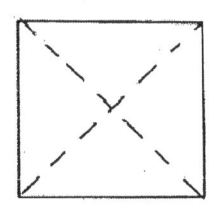

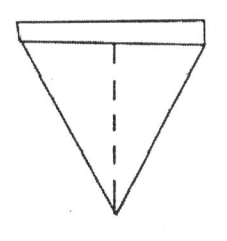

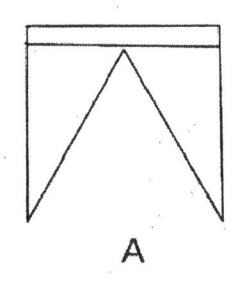

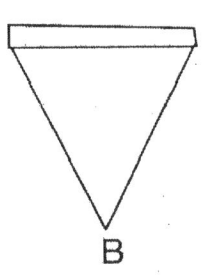

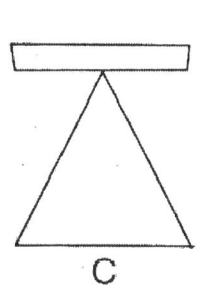

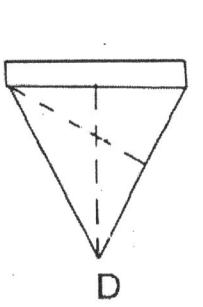

38.   38. _____

39.   39. _____

40.

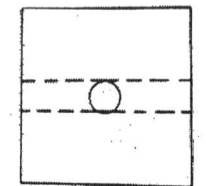

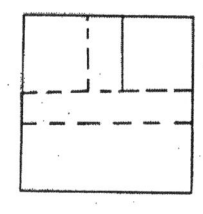

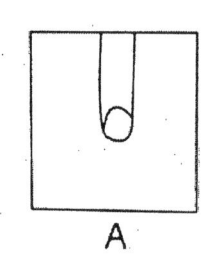

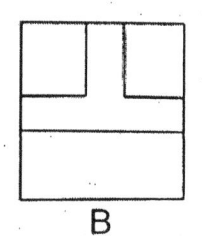

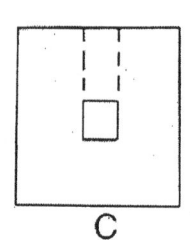

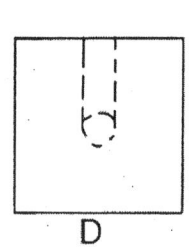

KEY (CORRECT ANSWERS)

1.	A	11.	B	21.	A	31.	B
2.	D	12.	A	22.	D	32.	C
3.	B	13.	C	23.	A	33.	C
4.	A	14.	B	24.	D	34.	C
5.	C	15.	A	25.	D	35.	A
6.	D	16.	E	26.	C	36.	B
7.	A	17.	G	27.	D	37.	A
8.	B	18.	F	28.	A	38.	B
9.	C	19.	D	29.	D	39.	A
10.	A	20.	A	30.	B	40.	C

EXAMINATION SECTION
TEST 1

DIRECTIONS: Each question or incomplete statement is followed by several suggested answers or completions. Select the one that BEST answers the question or completes the statement. *PRINT THE LETTER OF THE CORRECT ANSWER IN THE SPACE AT THE RIGHT.*

1. In pipe laying, the required width of trench in sand is less than that in clay because

   A. of the dilatancy of the sand
   B. the sand gives the pipe a more uniform support
   C. sand backfill puts less load upon the pipe
   D. of backfilling requirements
   E. it is easier to enlarge the trench for bell holes in sand

   1.____

2. A short post, 12 inches in diameter, is subjected to 75K applied 1" from the center. The maximum stress in the post, in lbs./sq.in., is MOST NEARLY

   A. 290   B. 995   C. 1,100   D. 1,260   E. 1,340

   2.____

3. Of the following, the geological feature which will have the LEAST effect on a foundation is

   A. stratification   B. foliation or cleavage
   C. striation   D. dip and strike
   E. faults

   3.____

4. In tall steel frame buildings, the columns are usually erected in lengths of

   A. 16 feet   B. 20 feet
   C. one story   D. two stories
   E. three stories

   4.____

5. The P.C. of a 7° curve is at Sta. 16+25.0. The deflection angle to Sta. 17+00 is

   A. 4° 29'   B. 3° 18'   C. 2° 38'   D. 1° 97'   E. 0° 42'

   5.____

6. Reverse curves on highways are customarily separated by tangents. Of the following, the BEST reason for this separation is

   A. to increase sight-distance
   B. to increase the radii of the curves
   C. to improve the appearance of the highway
   D. to avoid sudden changes in curvature
   E. concerned with superelevation

   6.____

7. The modulus of rupture of a wooden beam is

   A. greater than the ultimate strength in tension
   B. less than the ultimate strength in tension
   C. a function of the shearing strength if the beam is long
   D. less than the ultimate strength in compression
   E. independent of the cross-section of the beam

   7.____

8. Plain sedimentation is usually preferred to chemical precipitation in sewage treatment because

   A. disposition of the sludge resulting from chemical precipitation is difficult
   B. it removes a greater percentage of total suspended matter
   C. it removes a greater percentage of organic matter
   D. chemical precipitation always increases the pH concentration
   E. the resulting sludge is not putrescible

9. The strength of clay sewer pipe is NOT usually determined by a(n) _____ test.

   A. two-edge bearing   B. three-edge bearing
   C. sand bearing   D. *knife-edge*
   E. Izod or impact

10. The maximum moment that three moving loads of 6, 8, and 10 kips, from left to right, respectively, spaced 6 feet apart, can cause on a span of 30 feet is, in K feet,

    A. 110   B. 120.4   C. G. 152.6   D. 132.2   E. 95.1

11. In stream flow, a curve of rate of discharge versus gage height is known as a

    A. rating curve   B. mass diagram
    C. Rippl diagram   D. flood curve
    E. calibration curve

12. An inverted syphon carries a canal from one side of a valley at Elev. 100 to the other at Elev. 95. Assuming the coefficient of pipe friction is independent of diameter, the required diameter of pipe varies as

    A. $Q^{9/10}$ B. $Q^{4/5}$ C. $Q^{3/5}$ D. $Q^{2/5}$ E. $Q^{1/5}$

13. Two pipe lines carrying water are at the same elevation. Each is connected to a Bourdon Gage, the center of which is 4 feet vertically above the pipe center.
    If one gage registers 10 feet and the other minus 2 feet, the difference in pressure between the two pipes, in pounds per square inch, is about

    A. 6.9   B. 6.7   C. 5.9   D. 4.7   E. 3.9

14. The reason wooden beams bearing on brick walls are cut at the end with a mitre is

    A. a precaution in the event of fire
    B. so the inspector can be sure the beam is well seated
    C. to expose a fresh surface so that faulty wood may be detected
    D. that beams so cut may be placed more easily
    E. to make fire-stopping easier

15. Of the following conditions, shearing stress in the web of rolled steel beams is MOST likely to influence the choice of section when

    A. headroom requires the use of a section shallower than the most economical section
    B. the span is long and carries several uniformly spaced concentrated loads
    C. the deflection is small
    D. the span is long and carries two heavy concentrated loads, one near each support
    E. the span is long and uniformly loaded

16. The gridiron system of water distribution is

   A. preferable to the branching system with regard to fire protection
   B. only used in the largest cities
   C. less advantageous than the branching system because it requires a superimposed high pressure system
   D. being replaced by the branching system
   E. impractical in developments with many curved streets

16.____

17. An advantage of reinforced concrete beam and girder construction, as compared to flat slab construction, is

   A. greater fire resistance
   B. cheaper form work
   C. sprinkler layout is easier
   D. ventilation of rooms is easier
   E. none of the above

17.____

18. Activated sludge is sludge that

   A. is mixed mechanically
   B. has been *seeded*
   C. is stirred by air currents which give it a spiral motion
   D. is agitated in any one of several ways
   E. has been removed from a drying bed

18.____

19. In water purification, *aeration* is used to remove

   A. turbidity
   B. dissolved oxygen
   C. sediment
   D. organic material
   E. objectionable gases

19.____

20. The maximum unit stress to which a material may be subjected without suffering permanent deformation is known as the

   A. elastic limit
   B. yield strength
   C. proportional limit
   D. yield point
   E. commercial elastic limit

20.____

21. The distance in inches from the back of the short leg to the center of gravity of a 5" x 4" x 1/2" steel angle is APPROXIMATELY

   A. 0.80   B. 1.15   C. 1.40   D. 1.55   E. 1.60

21.____

22. A symmetrical triangular roof truss of four panels at 10 feet having a span of 40 feet between end supports and a rise of 10 feet carries a vertical load at the top center of 20,000 pounds.
The stress in the upper chord of the end panel, in pounds, is APPROXIMATELY

   A. 15,500   B. 19,500   C. 22,500   D. 26,500   E. 28,500

22.____

23. A short concrete column with an effective cross-section 30 inches square has two percent vertical steel reinforcing with proper tie.
Assuming f_c = 500 pounds per square inch, n = 15, the live load that can safely be carried by this column is
MOST NEARLY _____ pounds.

   A. 550,000   B. 575,000   C. 650,000   D. 675,000   E. 700,000

23.____

24. A welded cylindrical horizontal steel tank 36 inches in diameter is subjected to an internal pressure caused by 72-foot head of water. The ends of the tank are capped with hemispherical heads extending outward.
If the allowable tensile strength of the steel be taken as 18,000 lbs. per sq. in., the theoretical thickness of the heads should be, in inches,

   A. 0.735   B. 0.015   C. 0.475   D. 0.625   E. 0.375

25. Water flows from reservoir A, elev. 178, to reservoir B, elev. 106, through 3220 feet of 6" pipe; f = .02.
The velocity in the pipe, in ft./sec., is MOST NEARLY

   A. 1   B. 2   C. 3.5   D. 4.5   E. 6

26. Water is flowing through an open channel of triangular cross-section. The side slopes of the channel are 1:1. The water is 8 feet deep.
The hydraulic radius is

   A. 7.65   B. 6.40   C. 4.37   D. 3.59   E. 2.82

27. The building code of the large city specifies that bearing piles of wood shall not be spaced closer center to center, in inches, than

   A. 20   B. 24   C. 28   D. 32   E. 36

28. The four sides of a rectangular pier have a uniform batter of 2 inches per foot.
If the top of the pier is 4 feet by 10 feet and the pier is 12 feet high, the volume, to the NEAREST cubic foot, is

   A. 668   B. 880   C. 992   D. 745   E. 858

29. To lay out a line 170.00 feet long with a 100-foot tape which is actually 100.03 feet long, the taped distance should be

   A. 169.03   B. 169.95   C. 170.45   D. 170.50   E. 170.65

30. Of the following, the LEAST satisfactory method of preventing electrolysis in underground pipe lines near street railways is

   A. applying an insulating coat to the pipe
   B. using track joint bonds
   C. using track joint bonds and cross bonds
   D. using insulating joints on the pipe
   E. providing drains for the road bed

31. A uniformly loaded beam is continuous over four uniformly spaced supports, A, B, C, and D, reading from left to right.
If the support B settles slightly, the

   A. reaction at D decreases   B. reaction at C decreases
   C. moment at C decreases   D. moment at B increases
   E. reaction at A decreases

32. A flanged shaft coupling uses four 1-inch bolts equispaced on a circle 6 inches in radius. When the shaft is transmitting 300 horsepower at 200 r.p.m., the stress in the bolts, in pounds per square inch, is MOST NEARLY

   A. 5000   B. 4500   C. 4000   D. 3500   E. 3000

33. A simple beam on a 16 foot span carries a concentrated load of 5000 pounds at the mid-point.
If E is 1,600,000 pounds per square inch and I is 1728 inches fourth, the center deflection, in inches, is MOST NEARLY

   A. 0.27   B. 0.39   C. 0.47   D. 0.59   E. 0.67

34. The tensile efficiency of a riveted butt joint with adequate straps is a function of

   A. rivet diameter and plate width
   B. rivet diameter and plate thickness
   C. rivet diameter, plate width, and plate thickness
   D. plate width and thickness
   E. rivet value in double shear and in bearing

35. A 24-inch beam is made up of two 12-inch steel I-beams, the flanges in contact being riveted.
If the moment of inertia of a single 12-inch beam is 300 inches fourth and the cross-sectional area 15 square inches, the moment of inertia of the 24-inch beam is, in inches fourth, MOST NEARLY

   A. 2390   B. 1680   C. 1540   D. 920   E. 580

36. A distance taped on a 3 percent slope is 231.24 feet. The length, in feet, of the horizontal projection is

   A. 231.14   B. 231.07   C. 231.00   D. 230.93   E. 230.86

37. In running a closed level circuit, 50 set-ups were made. If each of the rod readings varied accidentally by plus or minus 0.003 feet from its correct value, the probable error of closure of the circuit is, in feet,

   A. 0.405   B. 0.325   C. 0.030   D. 0.015   E. 0.005

38. The dry weight of a cubic foot of sand is 104 pounds. The specific gravity of the sand grains is 2.60.
The submerged weight of a cubic foot of this sand in fresh water is, in pounds,

   A. 56   B. 60   C. 64   D. 68   E. 72

39. A street 40 feet wide with a parabolic cross-section has a crown of 6 inches at the center. The elevation of a point on the street surface 4 feet from the gutter is below the crown a distance, in inches, of

   A. 1.29   B. 2.73   C. 3.84   D. 4.51   E. 5.19

40. Line AB is extended to C with the transit set at A, a single, careful sight being taken. Subsequently, the transit is set at B, and C checked by a *double reverse*. All three points are at the same elevation.
If C fails to check the average of the *double reverse,* the transit is not in adjustment in that

   A. the horizontal axis is not perpendicular to the vertical axis
   B. the line of sight is not perpendicular to the horizontal axis
   C. either *a* or *b* or both may be the cause
   D. the axis of the objective slide does not coincide with the optical axis
   E. the line of sight is not parallel to the long bubble

41. The BEST material to use for a hydraulic-fill dam is a well-graded mixture ranging from

   A. gravel to fine silt   B. sand to clay
   C. coarse sand to silt   D. gravel to fine sand
   E. chips to ash

42. A round steel bar, one inch in diameter, is embedded 40 inches in concrete.
The unit tensile stress in the bar which will develop a bond stress of 100 pounds per square inch is, in pounds per square inch, about

   A. 19,000   B. 17,000   C. 16,000   D. 15,000   E. 13,000

43. The MOST important advantage of the Invar tape over the ordinary steel tape is it(s)

   A. will not rust
   B. high modulus of elasticity
   C. low coefficient of thermal expansion
   D. greater strength
   E. cheapness

44. Two clean steel pipes, one 12 inches in diameter, the other 6 inches in diameter, run from one reservoir to another in parallel.
If the slope of the hydraulic gradient is the same for the two pipes, the ratio of the discharge of the larger pipe to that of the smaller is about

   A. 5.6   B. 4.7   C. 3.9   D. 2.3   E. 1.1

45. The use of steel pipe to convey water is desirable because it

   A. never requires an inside coating
   B. can be fabricated by unskilled labor
   C. is not subject to electrolysis
   D. can carry large external loads
   E. does not have to be caulked

46. Reinforcing steel is usually shaped on the job

   A. by heating in a forge   B. by cutting and welding
   C. by hand bending   D. never
   E. on a bar-bending table

47. *Bulking* of sand   47.____

    A. is a maximum with a water content of about 6%
    B. is of no importance in concrete proportioning
    C. varies directly as the moisture content
    D. is greater for a coarse sand than a fine sand
    E. does not occur unless the sand contains over one-half gallon of water per cubic foot

48. The cinders used in *cinder concrete* should be   48.____

    A. thoroughly wetted down at least 24 hours before mixing
    B. thoroughly dry before mixing
    C. fine and powdery
    D. at least 50 percent uncombined carbon
    E. at least 50 percent combined carbon

49. Bank-run gravel ordinarily   49.____

    A. contains no sand
    B. contains too much sand to make a well-proportioned aggregate for concrete
    C. makes a well-proportioned aggregate for concrete
    D. contains too little sand to make a well-proportioned aggregate for concrete
    E. makes a good binder for macadam roads

50. The practical limit on the depth below water level to which the pneumatic caisson process may be carried is, in feet,   50.____

    A. 75   B. 85   C. 95   D. 110   E. 125

KEY (CORRECT ANSWERS)

1. D	11. A	21. D	31. A	41. B
2. C	12. D	22. C	32. A	42. C
3. C	13. A	23. B	33. A	43. C
4. D	14. A	24. B	34. A	44. A
5. C	15. D	25. E	35. B	45. E
6. E	16. A	26. E	36. A	46. E
7. A	17. E	27. B	37. C	47. A
8. A	18. B	28. B	38. C	48. A
9. E	19. E	29. B	39. C	49. B
10. D	20. A	30. A	40. D	50. D

TEST 2

DIRECTIONS: Each question or incomplete statement is followed by several suggested answers or completions. Select the one that BEST answers the question or completes the statement. *PRINT THE LETTER OF THE CORRECT ANSWER IN THE SPACE AT THE RIGHT.*

1. In earthwork, if two stations on a mass diagram have equal ordinates of like sign

    A. between the two stations, the volume of cut equals the volume of fill
    B. elevation of surface at the two stations is the same
    C. depth of cut or fill at the two stations is the same
    D. the distance between two stations equals the limit of economical haul

2. In the design of a reinforced concrete footing, which carries a reinforced concrete column, the distance from the face of the column to the critical section for shear is, in inches,

    A. kd   B. jd   C. d   D. zero

3. A major city building code permits reduction in the design live load of columns below the top floor as computed on the basis of design floor load because

    A. loads on lower floors offset moments created by loads on upper floors
    B. side sway is less when all floors are fully loaded
    C. lower columns are better braced
    D. it is unreasonable to expect all floors to be fully loaded at the same time

4. The term S2S means _____ two sides.

    A. shellac   B. sandpaper
    C. surfaced   D. split

5. The term *drop panel* is commonly used in

    A. plastering walls   B. plywood forms
    C. prefabricated housing   D. flat slab construction

6. In controlled concrete, the water-cement ratio is selected on the basis of

    A. consistency desired   B. proportion of aggregates
    C. type of aggregates   D. strength desired

7. A surcharge is usually MOST closely associated with

    A. highway superelevation   B. very long piles
    C. allowable fluid pressure D. retaining walls

8. Steam at 300 lb./sq.in. flows through a 1 ft. diameter pipe. The pipe walls are 1 in. thick. The unit circumferential stress is, in pounds per square inch,

    A. 900   B. 1800   C. 3200   D. 4800

9. On a topographic map, the symbol shown at the right represents
    A. tidal flat
    B. cultivated land
    C. orchard
    D. salt marsh

10. A square steel plate, 8 ft. on a side, is submerged in water with the top edge parallel to the water surface and 10 ft. below the surface.
    If the plate makes an angle of 30 with the water surface, the total pressure on the plate is, in pounds,

    A. 2688   B. 8649   C. 31,560   D. 47,900

    10.____

11. The stress in a steel bar 8 feet long, cross-sectional area 4 sq.in., rigidly set in a wall at both ends, due to a temperature rise of 30° F is, in pounds per square inch, (E = 30 x 10^6 lb./sq.in.; coefficient of expansion = 645 x 10^{-8})

    A. 628   B. 2775   C. 5800   D. 12,235

    11.____

12. The maximum unit stress up to which a material may be stressed without suffering permanent deformation when the stress is removed is called

    A. proportional limit   B. yield point
    C. elastic limit   D. ultimate stress

    12.____

13. The elongation of a steel bar, 100 feet long, cross-sectional area 1 sq.in., supported at one end and hanging vertically, due to its own weight is, in inches,
    (Steel weighs 490 lb./cu.ft.; E = 30 x 10^6 lb./sq.in.)

    A. .0019   B. .0068   C. .0077   D. .1586

    13.____

14. Lehoann's solution is used to determine

    A. orientation of a plane table
    B. longitude of station
    C. elevation of B.M. by method of least squares
    D. distances in a triangulation net

    14.____

15. In laying out a circular curve, the formula R vers $\frac{1}{2}$ I is used to determine the

    A. middle ordinate   B. tangent distance
    C. long chord   D. external distance

    15.____

16. The results of a survey of a closed traverse are as follows:

Line	Lat.	Dep.
AB	100.62	272.21
BC	153.27	422.16
CD	-322.14	19.23
DA	68.33	-713.50

    The magnitude of the linear error of closure is, in feet,

    A. .04   B. .07   C. .13   D. .15

    16.____

17. The notes for a three level section for a 20 feet wide roadway are

    $\frac{c\,7.5}{15}$ $\frac{c\,9}{0}$ $\frac{c\,12}{18}$

    The cross-sectional area of cut is, in square feet,

    A. 198   B. 246   C. 327   D. 415

    17.____

18. To determine the elevation of a point on the face of a building, a level was set up, a sight of 1.487 taken with a rod on the cap bolt of a hydrant, Elev. 39.470, and another sight taken on a tape with its zero end at the point (the tape stretching downward from the point).
    If the reading on the tape was 1.212, the elevation of the point is

    A. 42.169   B. 41.353   C. 40.457   D. 39.899

19. In taping, an accidental error may result from

    A. the tapeman unintentionally making a mistake
    B. the temperature being greater than that at which tape was standardized
    C. causes beyond control of the tapeman
    D. assuming slope distances to be horizontal distances

20. The maximum shearing stress in a wood joist 3 in. by 10 in., actual dimensions, simply supported at its ends on a 14 feet span, and sustaining a uniform load, including its own weight of 150 lb./ft. over the entire length is, in pounds per square inch,

    A. 39   B. 52   C. 68   D. 126

21. If the moment of inertia of a section is 1500 in. 4, and its area is 12 sq.in., the radius of gyration of the section is, in inches, APPROXIMATELY

    A. 11   B. 27   C. 49   D. 101

22. Of the following types of wall, which one is LEAST like the others in function? _____ wall.

    A. Curtain   B. Retaining   C. Spandrel   D. Wing

23. The bending moment at the ends of a beam rigidly supported at both ends and carrying a uniform load of w #/ft. throughout its entire length 1 ft. is, in ft.lbs.,

    A. $\dfrac{wl^2}{8}$ B. $\dfrac{wl}{10}$ C. $\dfrac{wl^2}{10}$ D. $\dfrac{wl^2}{12}$

24. The hydraulic radius of a rectangular canal 4 feet wide is 1.20.
    The depth of flow, in feet, is

    A. 1.6   B. 2.1   C. 2.6   D. 3.0

25. The dynamic pressure into which the kinetic energy of water is transformed when the valve at the outlet of a pipe is suddenly closed is called

    A. velocity head   B. static head
    C. water hammer   D. hydraulic gradient

26. The length of a 3/8" fillet weld required to resist a shear of 12,000 lbs., if the allowable shearing stress is 13,000 lb./sq.in., is, in inches,

    A. 1.97   B. 2.31   C. 2.77   D. 3.48

4 (#2)

27. Bridge trusses are built with a slight camber in order to

   A. make erection easier
   B. avoid sag under load
   C. eliminate secondary stresses
   D. reduce tension in lower chord

28. The formula for determining the value of *n* in concrete design, as given by the A.C.I. and a major city building code is

   A. $\dfrac{3000}{f'c}$ B. $\dfrac{fs}{f'c}$ C. $\dfrac{fs}{fc}$ D. $\dfrac{Es}{fc \times 10^3}$

29. In reinforced concrete design with fs = 18,000 lb./sq.in., fc = 1000 lb./sq.in. and n = 12, the value of k is

   A. .389   B. .396   C. .400   D. .420

30. Water flows through a 2" ⌀ orifice in the side of a tank under a head of 20 ft. If Cd = .60, the quantity of discharge is, in cfs,

   A. .47   B. .91   C. 1.27   D. 239.4

31. Water discharges through a turbine at the rate of 60,000 cfm under a head of 100 ft. If the efficiency of the turbine is 70%, the horsepower developed by the turbine is

   A. 646   B. 7,950   C. 21,300   D. 44,440

32. Stirrups are used in concrete construction to

   A. support reinforcing rods
   B. reinforce concrete for the diagonal tension component of shear
   C. hold forms together
   D. prevent cracking of concrete due to changes of temperature

33. In the design of a steel member in tension, rivet holes must be deducted to obtain the net section.
   This is not done when the member is in compression because

   A. rivet holes are smaller
   B. formulae for design of compression members reduce allowable stress
   C. rivets can be placed more efficiently
   D. rivets are assumed to fill the holes

34. In a specific gravity determination, the weight of a flask full of water is 390.0 grams. The weight of the same flask filled with water and 96.2 grams of sand is 450.0 grams. The specific gravity of the sand is

   A. 2.58   B. 2.66   C. 2.74   D. 2.82

35. A soil has a void ratio of 0.80 and a specific gravity of solids of 2.67.
   The total weight (including the water) of a saturated cubic foot of this soil is, in pounds,

   A. 173.4   B. 120.4   C. 111.1   D. 72.7

36. The loss in head per 1,000 feet in a 12-inch water pipe is 9 feet, and the friction factor, f, is 0.0161.
    The velocity of flow in the pipe is, in feet per second,

    A. 6.0   B. 8.1   C. 13.9   D. 18.3

Questions 37-40.

DIRECTIONS: Questions 37 through 40 refer to the truss shown below.

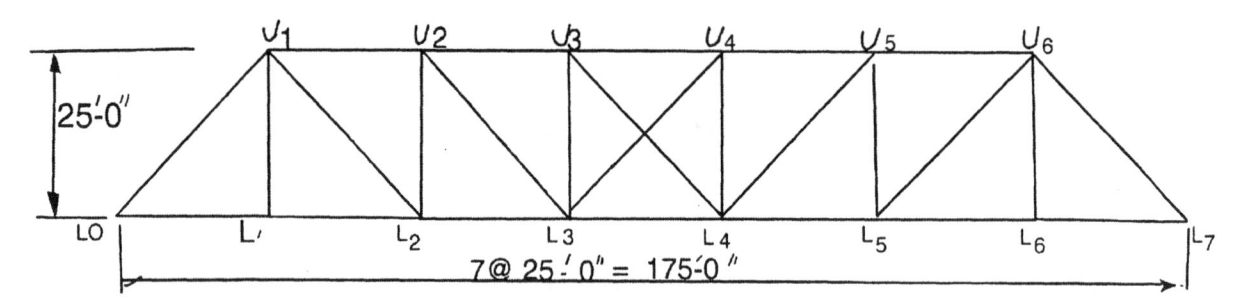

37. If a uniformly distributed live load of 2 kips per foot extends over the entire length of the truss, the live load shear in panel L_2L_3 is, in kips,

    A. 150   B. 100   C. 50   D. 0

38. If the stress in U_2L_2 is -150 kips (compression) and in L_1L_2 +300 kips (tension), the stress in L_2L_3 is, in kips,

    A. +619   B. +450   C. +324   D. +108

39. For a uniformly distributed live load, the maximum tensile stress in member U_2L_3 will occur when the truss is loaded from the

    A. right up to panel point L_3
    B. right up to a point between L_3 and L_2
    C. left up to panel point L_2
    D. left up to a point between L_2 and L_3

40. For a uniformly distributed live load, the maximum tensile stress in member U_2L_2 will occur when the truss is loaded from the left up to

    A. panel point L_3
    B. panel point L_2
    C. a point midway between L_2 and L_3
    D. a point 8'4" from L_2 in panel L_2L_3

KEY (CORRECT ANSWERS)

1.	A	11.	C	21.	A	31.	B
2.	C	12.	C	22.	A	32.	B
3.	D	13.	B	23.	D	33.	D
4.	C	14.	A	24.	D	34.	B
5.	D	15.	A	25.	C	35.	B
6.	D	16.	C	26.	D	36.	A
7.	D	17.	B	27.	B	37.	C
8.	B	18.	A	28.	A	38.	B
9.	D	19.	C	29.	C	39.	B
10.	D	20.	B	30.	A	40.	D

TEST 3

DIRECTIONS: Each question or incomplete statement is followed by several suggested answers or completions. Select the one that BEST answers the question or completes the statement. *PRINT THE LETTER OF THE CORRECT ANSWER IN THE SPACE AT THE RIGHT.*

1. A grit chamber is an enlarged channel through which sewage flows

    A. while being screened
    B. with a velocity of from 0.6 to 2.6 feet per minute
    C. with a velocity reduced to cause heavy solids to be deposited
    D. depositing grit which decomposes in the bottom
    E. in recessed chambers

2. An end post is

    A. a long column
    B. a diagonal compression member
    C. a short column
    D. the end member of a compression chord on a through truss
    E. the outside vertical member of a bent

3. A strut is

    A. a long column
    B. a diagonal compression member
    C. a wide column
    D. the end member of a compression chord on a through truss
    E. the outside vertical member of a bent

4. Of the following items, the one which has NOTHING to do with stadia computations is

    A. Cox computer   B. Beaman arc
    C. stadia slide rule   D. stadia tables
    E. gradienter

5. In laying up a brick wall, bond refers to the

    A. adhesive property of the mortar
    B. anchors or ties which hold a brick veneer wall to a building
    C. beam anchors
    D. use of bats or half bricks
    E. use of headers and stretchers

6. In a reinforced concrete building of the slab beam and girder type, architectural considerations limit the size of one beam to such an extent that the concrete stress in that beam is excessive.
   The MOST practical solution is to

    A. ignore the architectural considerations
    B. use a better quality concrete throughout the building
    C. use a better quality concrete in the beam under consideration
    D. increase the required tension steel
    E. provide compression steel

7. A reinforced concrete beam 10" wide x 12" effective depth, on a simple span of 12'0", is reinforced in tension only with three 1/2" square rods.
If the allowable steel and concrete stresses are 18,000 and 600 p.s.i., respectively, and K is 1/3, the maximum uniform load that the beam can carry (including its own weight) is, in pounds per foot,

   A. 592   B. 623   C. 667   D. 689   E. 714

8. A statically indeterminate structure

   A. is one to which the equations of static equilibrium do not apply
   B. is statically indeterminate because of secondary stresses
   C. requires more material than an equivalent statically determinate structure because of the uncertainty of the exact values of the stresses in the former
   D. is statically indeterminate because of rigid joints
   E. requires at least one equation in addition to those of static equilibrium, for a solution

9. A masonry wall with a rectangular cross-section is 14 feet high.
If water stands behind the wall two feet below its top and if the masonry weighs 150 pounds per cubic foot, the required width of the wall to just prevent overturning is, in feet,

   A. 4.14   B. 4.54   C. 5.24   D. 5.84   E. 6.04

10. If the hydraulic radius of a stream is close to unity, the cross-section of the stream is

    A. semi-circular   B. square
    C. triangular   D. deep and narrow
    E. wide and shallow

11. In column formulae, allowance for accidental eccentricity

    A. is made in the factor of safety
    B. is a function of length
    C. is not made
    D. depends only on the section of the column
    E. must be estimated by the designer

12. An emergency pipe line connecting two reservoirs consists of 3,000 feet of 16" pipe followed by 6,000 feet of 24" pipe which leads into the lower reservoir.
The hydraulic grade line for this pipe

    A. does not drop continuously in the direction of flow
    B. drops continuously in the direction of flow
    C. is affected by the ground profile
    D. is affected by the pipe profile
    E. never rises in the direction of flow

13. The use of several pipes rather than one pipe in an inverted syphon carrying a sewer under a subway is considered good practice because

    A. it helps prevent deposition in the syphon
    B. it reduces the headroom required
    C. several small pipes are cheaper than one big one
    D. the resultant head loss is smaller
    E. it reduces the velocity of flow

14. If the objective lens of a transit telescope is focused to give an observer the clearest possible view of an object,

    A. no parallax can exist
    B. the proper way to eliminate parallax would involve refocusing of both objective and eyepiece
    C. parallax should be ignored
    D. any error due to parallax can be eliminated by a direct and a reversed sight
    E. nothing can be done to eliminate any parallax that may exist

15. The ground rod at Sta. 18+00 is 6.2. If the grade rod is 8.8,

    A. the fill is 3.7
    B. the cut is 14.8
    C. the fill is 15.0
    D. there is no way of telling whether there is cut or fill of 14.8
    E. there is no way of telling whether there is cut or fill of 3.7

16. In a circular curve of radius R and central angle I, the distance $R(\frac{1}{\cos \frac{1}{2}} - 1)$ is used to locate the

    A. point of curvature
    B. point of intersection or vertex
    C. center of the curve from the vertex
    D. midpoint of the chord of the circular curve
    E. midpoint of the long chord

17. A line 442.25 feet long is to be laid out with a 100-foot steel tape which is 100.07 feet long.
    The taped length which should be laid out in the field is

    A. 441.94   B. 441.99   C. 442.04   D. 442.09   E. 442.14

18. Water flows from reservoir A, Elev. 100, to reservoir B through 16,100 feet of 12-inch pipe.
    If the friction factor, f, is 0.02 and the flow 3.14 cubic feet per second, the elevation of the water surface in reservoir B is MOST NEARLY

    A. 32   B. 28   C. 24   D. 20   E. 16

19. The area bounded by the X-axis, the ordinates x = 1 and x = 4, and the curve $y = x^2-6x-7$ is

    A. 45   B. 41   C. 37   D. 33   E. 29

20. A tie rod 20'0" long and one inch in diameter, fastened to rigid supports at its ends, is under a tension of 10,000 p.s.i. when the temperature is 68° F.
If the temperature rises to 98° F, the tension in the rod will be MOST NEARLY, in p.s.i.,

   A. 4140 B. 5960 C. 7235 D. 10,800 E. 13,444

21. A 14 WF 246 section has a cross-sectional area, in square inches, of about

   A. 63.5 B. 72.5 C. 76.5 D. 80.5 E. 84.5

22. A load of lumber consists of 25 pieces 4" x 6" x 15'3". The total F.B.M. is MOST NEARLY

   A. 8160 B. 6640 C. 762 D. 868 E. 2155

23. In concrete work, the slump test

   A. is used to determine time of initial set
   B. may be used as a rough check of the water-cement ratio
   C. could give identical results for two concrete mixes of entirely different water-cement ratios
   D. is used in the field only after the concrete has proper workability
   E. is gradually being replaced by the Vicat apparatus

24. A gusset plate is attached to one flange of an H-section column by four rivets which lie at the corners of a 6" x 8" rectangle with the 6" side horizontal. The plate carries a vertical concentrated load with action line 20 inches to the right of the center of the rivet group. Lettering the rivets a, b, c, and d in clockwise order starting at the upper lefthand corner, the maximum total rivet stress occurs in

   A. a and b   B. b and d   C. b *only*
   D. b and c   E. c and d

25. A steel I-beam with a section modulus of 120 inches cubed is to carry a uniformly-distributed load including its own weight on a simple span of 12'0". The maximum allowable fibre stress is 16,000 p.s.i.
Of the following loads, in pounds per foot (including the weight of the beam), the largest load the beam can carry is

   A. 767 B. 2890 C. 8800 D. 19,705 E. 24,664

26. A flat plate carrying a tensile load of 24,000 pounds is to be connected to a gusset plate by means of 5/16" fillet welds.
If the allowable unit shearing stress on welds is 11,300 p.s.i., the total length of weld required, in inches, is MOST NEARLY

   A. 27.4 B. 17.3 C. 9.6 D. 7.7 E. 6.6

27. The latitudes and departures of a closed traverse are as follows:

Line	Latitude	Departure
AB	+1000	0
BC	0	+1000
CA	-998	-998

   The error of closure is MOST NEARLY

   A. 1:1200 B. 1:1000 C. 1:800 D. 1:500 E. 1:300

28. The flanges and web of an H-section 12" wide by 12" deep are each 1" thick. The moment of inertia of the section about an axis through the center of gravity and parallel to the flanges is, in inches fourth,

    A. 263   B. 387   C. 595   D. 811   E. 929

29. A circular gate 4' in diameter lies in a vertical plane with its top 4' below the water surface.
    The total water pressure on one side of the gate, in pounds, is MOST NEARLY

    A. 800   B. 3200   C. 3700   D. 4700   E. 4500

30. Two 3/8" plates under a tension of 50,000 lbs. are lap riveted with 7/8" rivets. Allowable unit values of rivets are 15,000 lbs. p.s.i. for shear and 32,000 lbs. p.s.i. for bearing.
    The number of 7/8" rivets required for this joint is

    A. 1   B. 2   C. 3   D. 4   E. 6

31. A Warren-type deck truss with a span of 60' 0" has 3 panels at 20' 0" and is 20' 0" deep. Under a uniform load of one kip per foot per truss, the maximum stress in the compression chord is, in kips,

    A. 40   B. 35   C. 30   D. 20   E. 10

32. The allowable tensile and bond stresses in reinforcing bars for concrete are 16,000 and 100 p.s.i., respectively. The depth of embedment, in inches, required to develop the allowable tensile strength of a 3/4" diameter bar is

    A. 50   B. 30   C. 20   D. 10   E. 5

33. A sedimentation tank is an enlarged channel through which sewage flows

    A. while being screened
    B. with a velocity of from 0.5 to 2.5 feet per minute
    C. with a velocity reduced to cause heavy solids to be deposited
    D. depositing grit which decomposes in the bottom
    E. in recessed chambers

34. A level is set up so that a Philadelphia rod reads 4.00 on B.M.A., elev. 90.00. A tape rod is then set to read 0.00 at B.M.A. and reads 0.84 at point B.
    The elevation of point B is

    A. computed from the H.I.   B. 90.84
    C. 90.37   D. 88.74
    E. 87.14

35. A Proctor compaction test is usually MOST closely associated with the use in the field of a

    A. drag line   B. bulldozer
    C. pile driver   D. sheep's-foot roller
    E. post-hole digger

36. The MOST important consideration in the design of a building foundation resting on a deep clay layer is concerned with

    A. minimum settlement
    B. differential settlement
    C. length of construction period
    D. weather conditions during construction
    E. shape of footing

36.____

37. The discharge of a stream varies from 0.1 to 10.0 cubic feet per second, with a mean discharge of about 0.3 c.f.s. The BEST type of weir to measure flow in this stream is

    A. suppressed rectangular   B. contracted rectangular
    C. trapezoidal   D. submerged
    E. triangular

37.____

38. A peg test on a transit has been completed.
    The first step in the actual adjustment based on the result of the test involves movement of

    A. a diagonally-opposite pair of foot screws
    B. the cross-hair ring
    C. the long bubble by means of the bubble-adjusting screw
    D. the telescope about the horizontal axis
    E. the plate bubbles

38.____

39. A steel specimen was tested to destruction in a tension test in which no extensometer was used.
    Results which could be reported would include

    A. elastic limit   B. yield point
    C. modulus of elasticity   D. proportional limit
    E. initial set

39.____

40. Of the five items following, which one bears the LEAST relationship to the other four?

    A. Shore   B. Needle
    C. Pretest pile   D. Underpinning
    E. Pile loading test

40.____

KEY (CORRECT ANSWERS)

1. C	11. B	21. B	31. D
2. D	12. A	22. C	32. B
3. B	13. A	23. C	33. B
4. E	14. B	24. D	34. B
5. E	15. C	25. C	35. D
6. E	16. C	26. C	36. B
7. A	17. A	27. A	37. E
8. E	18. D	28. D	38. D
9. A	19. A	29. D	39. B
10. E	20. A	30. E	40. E

EXAMINATION SECTION
TEST 1

DIRECTIONS: Each question or incomplete statement is followed by several suggested answers or completions. Select the one that BEST answers the question or completes the Statement. *PRINT THE LETTER OF THE CORRECT ANSWER IN THE SPACE AT THE RIGHT.*

1. The P.C. of a 7-degree curve is at Sta 16 + 25.0. The deflection angle to Sta 17 + 00 is *most clearly*   1.____

   A. 5°15'   B. 3°30'   C. 2°38'   D. 1°45'

2.   2.____

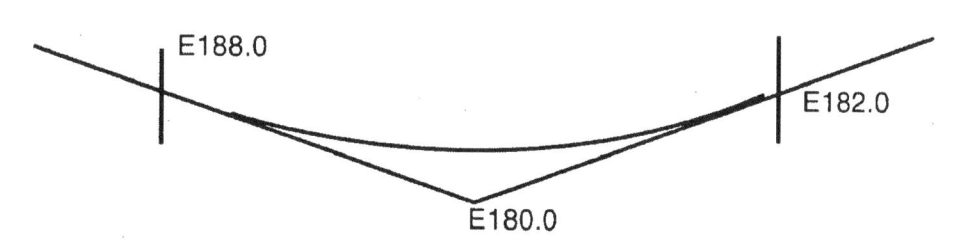

   The above sketch shows a parabolic vertical curve. The tangents are of equal length. The elevation of the center of the curve is

   A. 85.0   B. 84.5   C. 83.5   D. 82.5

3. The volume of the solid shown below is in cubic inches, *most nearly*   3.____

   A. 42   B. 40   C. 38   D. 36

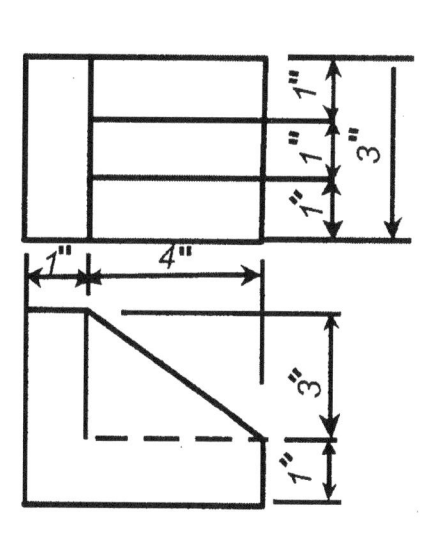

4. The volume of the solid shown below is, *most nearly*,

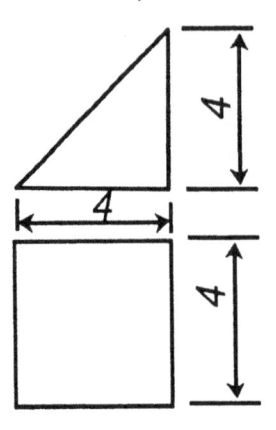

A. 64   B. 32   C. $32\sqrt{2}$ D. $16\sqrt{2}$

5. In trigonometry, the expression $1-2\sin^2 x$ is equal to

A. sin 2 x   B. cos 2 x   C. sin 1/2 x   D. cos 1/2 x

6. A survey was made of a five-sided piece of property as shown below. Four of the angles were measured as noted on the diagram.
The fifth should be in degrees, *most nearly*,

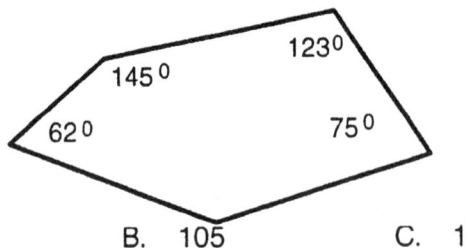

A. 45   B. 105   C. 135   D. 35

7. The diagonal of a square is $\sqrt{72}$.
The area of the square is, in square feet, *most nearly*,

A. 36   B. 48   C. 64   D. 72

8. A square whose side is *a* has the same area as a rectangle whose sides are *b* and *c*. Of the following statements, the one that is TRUE is

A. $a = \sqrt{bc}$ B. b = a c   C. $b = \sqrt{ac}$ D. a b = b c

9. The mathematical formula that will give the MOST accurate results in determining the area of an irregular plane surface is:

A. Simpson's Rule
B. Horizontal Rule
C. Pappus' Theorum
D. Average End Area Method

10. If $y = x^3$, $\frac{d^2y}{dx^2}$ is equal to

   A. 6x B. $3x^2$ C. $\frac{x^5}{20}$ D. $2x^3$

11. The most probable value of a series of measurements of the same quantity made under similar conditions is the arithmetic mean of the quantity. A line was measured four times and the recorded lengths of the line are: 913.35, 913.36, 913.42, 913.43.
    The MOST probable length of the line is

   A. 913.36 B. 913.38 C. 913.39 D. 913.40

12. The bearing of line C D in the traverse shown below is

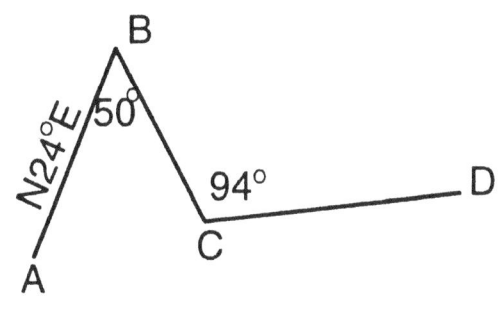

   A. N 78°E B. N 68°E C. S 26°E D. N 78°W

13. The stadia method is commonly used in _____ surveys.

   A. topographic B. triangulation
   C. photogrammetric D. geodetic

14. A surveyor is assigned to check the structural steel of a tall steel frame building. The steel is past the first floor.
    Of the following, the MOST important factor to be checked is the _____ of the _____ columns.

   A. plumbness; interior B. plumbness; exterior
   C. elevation; interior D. elevation; exterior

15. It is necessary to plot a circular curve on a drawing. If the radius or center is not known, the number of points on the circumference needed to determine the curve is

   A. 1 B. 2 C. 3 D. 4

16. In ordinary profile leveling, there

   A. are more foresights than backsights
   B. are more backsights than foresights
   C. are as many foresights as backsights
   D. may be more or less foresights than backsights

17.

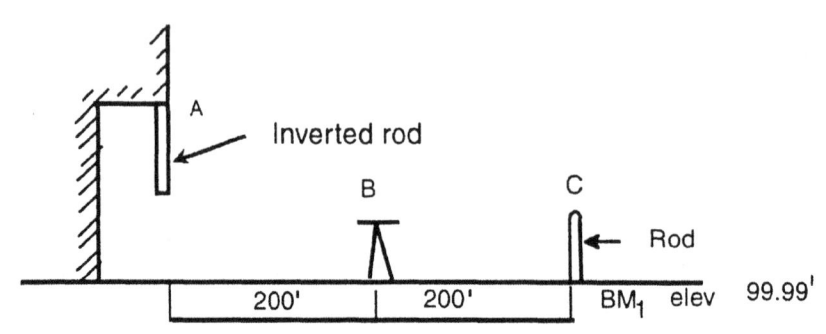

The rod reading at C = 4.39', and the rod reading at A = 4.39'. The elevation of point A is

A. 99.99'   B. 108.77'   C. 4.39'   D. 104.38'

18. The coordinates of point A are (N 780, E 660) and the coordinates of point B are (N 650, E 620). Point B is _____ of A.

A. Northeast
B. Northwest
C. Southeast
D. Southwest

19. The following set of notes was taken on the closed level circuit EFG. The elevation of bench mark E is 35.47. There are no errors in levelling.

Sta	BS	HI	FS	Elev.
E	6:29			35.47
F	4:20		5:05	
G	3:21		6:02	
F				
E				

The elevation of BMG is
A. 42.73   B. 34.89   C. 43.15   D. 38.10

20. If the bench mark elevation is 6.42 and the B. S. reading is 5.50, the reading that should be set on the rod as an F. S. reading to set an elevation of 8.23 is in feet, *most nearly*,

A. 3.69   B. 7.31   C. 9.15   D. 11.92

21. When transferring line and grade from the surface to a deep tunnel,

A. a small error in transferring grade to the bottom of the shaft will cause a large error in grade in the tunnel
B. a small error in transferring line to the bottom of the shaft will cause a large error in line in the tunnel
C. trigonometric leveling is used to transfer grade into the tunnel
D. reciprocal leveling is used to transfer grade into the tunnel

22. The invert of a sewer is a (the)

A. syphon
B. bottom of the outside surface
C. bottom of the inside surface
D. top of the inside surface

23. The datum in one borough is 1.725' above mean sea level. The elevation of a point in the borough is minus 2.50. The datum in another borough is 2.725' above mean sea level. The elevation of the point with reference to the latter datum is

    A. -4.225   B. -3.225   C. 1.50   D. -3.50

23.____

24.

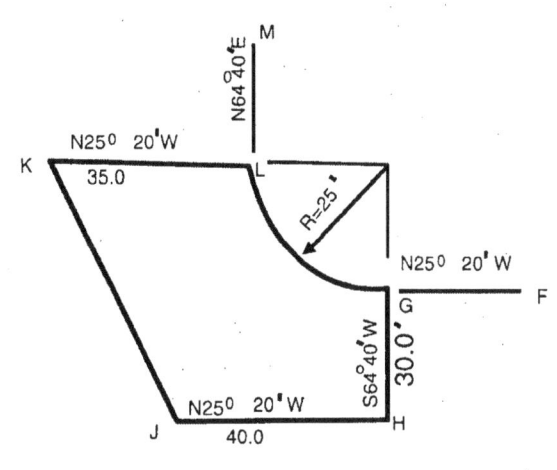

The area of the enclosed figure is, in square feet, *most nearly*,
    A. 2100   B. 2260   C. 2370   D. 2450

24.____

25. The sin $(x + 60°)$ is equal to

    A. $\sin(30 - x)$ B. $\sin(30 + x)$
    C. $\cos(30 - x)$ D. $\cos(30 + x)$

25.____

KEY (CORRECT ANSWERS)

1.	C	11.	C
2.	D	12.	B
3.	D	13.	A
4.	B	14.	B
5.	B	15.	C
6.	C	16.	A
7.	A	17.	B
8.	A	18.	D
9.	A	19.	B
10.	A	20.	A

    21. B
    22. C
    23. D
    24. B
    25. C

TEST 2

DIRECTIONS: Each question or incomplete statement is followed by several suggested answers or completions. Select the one that BEST answers the question or completes the Statement. *PRINT THE LETTER OF THE CORRECT ANSWER IN THE SPACE AT THE RIGHT.*

1. The shape of the main cables on a suspension bridge is, *most nearly*, a(n)
    A. parabola
    B. hyperbola
    C. circular segment
    D. straight line

    1.___

2. The area of a rectangular plot that scales 3" x 4 1/2" on a map whose scale is 1" =60' is, in square feet, *most nearly,*
    A. 13 1/2
    B. 48,600
    C. 810
    D. 720

    2.___

3. To a water tank that is 1/4 full, 250 gallons of water are added. The tank, then, is 1/3 full. The capacity of the tank is, in gallons, *most nearly,*
    A. 12,000
    B. 3,000
    C. 1,000
    D. 750

    3.___

4. A random line is used in surveying when

    A. it is desired to connect two distant points with a straight line when the points are not intervisible
    B. a trial line is needed to determine the best method of running a survey
    C. it is necessary to set the transit on line
    D. the actual distance between two points is too great to be sighted from one end of the line

    4.___

5. Of the following numbers, the one that is NOT a rational number is
    A. -1 5/8
    B. i^2
    C. $\sqrt{2}$
    D. 0

    5.___

6. If the magnetic declination is 12°W, and the magnetic bearing of a line is N34°E, then the *true bearing* of the line is
    A. N58° E
    B. N46° E
    C. N22° E
    D. N10° E

    6.___

7. (5+3i) (5-3i) is
    A. 34
    B. 25-9i
    C. $25-6i-9i^2$
    D. 16

    7.___

8. $\cos^2 x = 1/2$. x equals, in degrees
    A. 15
    B. 30
    C. 45
    D. 60

    8.___

9. The deflection angle required to lay out a 50-foot chord of a 3°00' circular curve is, *most nearly,*
    A. 0°45'
    B. 1°30'
    C. 2°15'
    D. 3°00'

    9.___

70

2 (#2)

10.

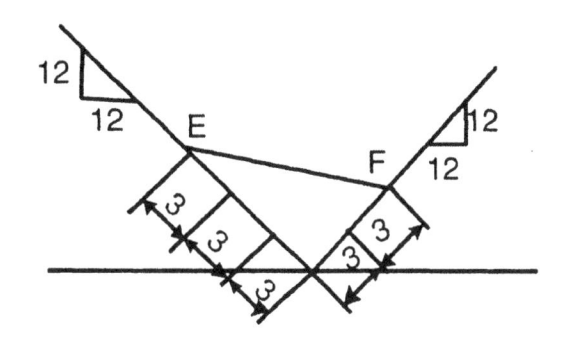

Distance EF is, in inches, *most nearly,*
   A. 10 7/16   B. 10 9/16   C. 10 4/16   D. 10 13/16

11. If in the binary system of notation,
$$1 = 1$$
$$2 = 10$$
$$3 = 11,$$
the number six would be represented in the binary system by the number

   A. 100   B. 101   C. 110   D. 11

12. The *third* term in the expansion $(a+b)^6$ is

   A. $15a^4b^2$ B. $20a^4b^2$ C. $30a^4b^2$ D. $10a^4b^2$

13. 48 x 12 is equal to

   A. $3^3 \cdot 4^2$ B. $4^3 \cdot 3^2$ C. $4^4 \cdot 3^2$ D. $3^4 \cdot 4^2$

14. For a given angle *x*, which of the following is CORRECT?

   A. $\tan^2 x = 1 + \sec^2 x$
   B. $\sin^2 x + \cos^2 x = 1$
   C. $\tan x = \dfrac{\cos x}{\sin x}$
   D. $\sec x = \dfrac{1}{\sin x}$

15. If $x = 1$ and $x^3 + x^2 + x^1 + x + x^{-1} = y$, y equals

   A. 2   B. 3   C. 4   D. 5

16. A specification for a heavy construction job reads, in part: All timber used for sheeting, shoring, bracing or other temporary purposes shall be sound and free from any defects that may impair its strength.
According to good practice, the method by which the above provision is enforced is that the engineer in charge or an assigned inspector

   A. sees that the appropriate grade stamp appears on each piece
   B. checks for compliance by visual inspection of the lumber used
   C. prohibits use of previously used lumber
   D. reports the defects to the materials inspection division for a ruling

17. When a membrane waterproofing is referred to, it means the

   A. adding of a waterproofing ingredient to the fresh concrete
   B. thorough draining of the foundation
   C. coating of the structure with waterproof material
   D. using of a dense concrete mix

18. The welding symbol _____ designates a _____ weld.

   A. fillet
   B. butt
   C. spot
   D. plug

19.

   The value of the weight W is, in pounds, *most nearly,*
   A. 800   B. 850   C. 900   D. 950

20. A squad leader on design work in the office should assign work to the members of his group so that

   A. each member will get the work he likes best to do
   B. one group will usually prepare designs and another group will usually check
   C. older members of the group will get the more difficult assignments
   D. each member of the group will get the work for which he is best suited

21. Water flowing into the top of a tank from pipe A can fill the tank in 4 minutes. Water from pipe B alone can fill the tank in 6 minutes.
If both pipes are used, the time in which the tank will be filled is, in minutes, *most nearly,*

   A. 2.0   B. 2.8   C. 2.6   D. 2.4

22. Vermiculite is used as an aggregate in plaster PRIMARILY because of its

   A. quicksetting characteristics
   B. light weight
   C. workability
   D. low cost

23. In the formula, $H_f = f \dfrac{1}{d} \dfrac{v^2}{2g}$ the value of f for smooth d v2 cast iron pipes, is, *most nearly,*

   A. 0.02   B. 1.486   C. 0.14   D. 100.0

24. Drop manholes are

    A. sometimes used when streets have steep slopes
    B. never used in an original sewer design
    C. not used in flat topography
    D. usually shallower than regular manholes

25. In a unit price contract,

    A. payment to the contractor is based upon the total quantities of the various items comprising the work
    B. the agreement stipulates a specified sum to cover the cost of the entire job
    C. payment is based on the Engineer News-Record construction costs index
    D. contractor is required to furnish labor and material bills to establish the cost of the job

---

KEY (CORRECT ANSWERS)

1.	A	11.	C
2.	B	12.	A
3.	B	13.	B
4.	A	14.	B
5.	C	15.	D
6.	C	16.	B
7.	A	17.	C
8.	C	18.	A
9.	A	19.	C
10.	D	20.	D

21. D
22. B
23. A
24. A
25. A

EXAMINATION SECTION
TEST 1

DIRECTIONS: Each question or incomplete statement is followed by several suggested answers or completions. Select the one that BEST answers the question or completes the statement. *PRINT THE LETTER OF THE CORRECT ANSWER IN THE SPACE AT THE RIGHT.*

1. A general contractor, on a lump sum building construction job, is required to submit a breakdown of his estimate in order to

   A. prevent collusion in bidding
   B. serve as a guide in checking his monthly estimates for payment
   C. enable designers to prepare budget estimates for proposed work
   D. enable designers to compare it with their estimate of cost of the job

   1.____

2. Of the following, the index MOST often applied to indicate the strength of sewage is

   A. odor
   B. biochemical oxygen demand
   C. foaming
   D. turbidity

   2.____

3. Of the following, the MINIMUM amount of cover required for water mains in the city is *primarily* determined by the

   A. traffic shock loads
   B. pressure in the main
   C. depth of rock below street surfaces
   D. depth of frost

   3.____

4. The one of the following in which an inspector of pile driving has the MOST interest during driving wood piles is

   A. weather conditions
   B. mushrooming of the head
   C. penetration
   D. water table location

   4.____

5. A bidder on a public job is required to furnish a bid bond to guarantee that he will

   A. sign a contract if awarded the job
   B. complete the job on schedule
   C. pay the mechanics who will work on the job
   D. pay the subcontractors whom he will employ to work on the job

   5.____

Questions 6-7.

DIRECTIONS: Questions 6 and 7 refer to the following diagram.

A section through a roof appears as shown below.

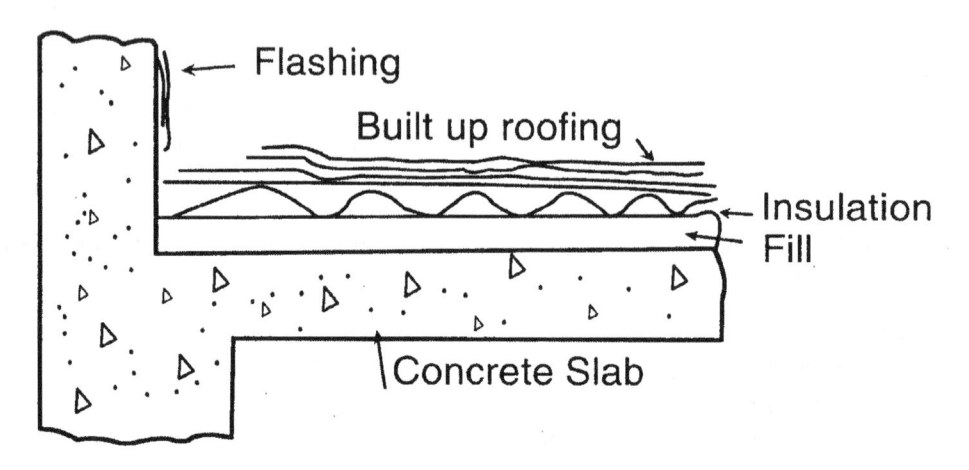

Diagram: Cross-section showing Flashing, Built up roofing, Insulation Fill, and Concrete Slab.

6. Of the following, the MAIN purpose of the fill is to

   A. provide a smooth base for the insulation
   B. reduce sound transmission
   C. absorb impact of roof loads
   D. facilitate drainage

7. Of the following, the material composition of the fill is *most likely*

   A. one-inch cinder block B. compacted sand
   C. Wood D. lightweight concrete

8. An excavation for a building in the downtown area is kept dry by pumping from a sump. It would be a danger signal to an inspector if

   A. the pumped water is always clear
   B. after a heavy rain, the pumped water is muddy
   C. the pumped water is continually muddy
   D. the rate of pumping decreases materially with time

9. The PRIMARY reason for placing reinforced steel in concrete is that concrete is weak in

   A. torsion   B. tension   C. compression   D. bond

10. Of the following types of construction, the one that would *most likely* be paid for on a lump sum basis would be a new

    A. subway
    B. sewer
    C. street paving and regulating
    D. building

11. Of the following situations, the one in which it is MOST important to have a fire extinguisher on hand is when

    A. welding a broken bracket on a bulldozer
    B. welding a structural steel field connection
    C. burning reinforcing steel in place before a concrete pour
    D. bending reinforced steel at the bar bending machine

12. Wall plaster is composed of

    A. sand, cement, gypsum, water
    B. coarse aggregate, gypsum, water
    C. sand, gypsum, water
    D. lime, gypsum, cement, water

13. Of the following, the LEAST important factor in establishing grades for a new urban street is existing

    A. manholes
    B. underground utilities
    C. sewers
    D. sidewalks

14. The activated sludge treatment process reduces organic matter in the sewage to inorganic matter PRIMARILY by

    A. electrolysis
    B. sedimentation
    C. bacteriological action
    D. catalytic action

15. Assume that you are a party chief on a preliminary survey for a major construction project with a four-man party. Two of your men are able to operate the transit. You consider one of these men an expert, while the other is lacking in experience. You have been following a policy of assigning each man to the transit on alternate days. You get a call from the design department to furnish a check on a series of angles as quickly as possible. On this day, it is the inexperienced man's turn at the transit. You should

    A. allow the inexperienced man to run the gun for that is the only way he can become experienced
    B. have the experienced man run the gun and explain the need for speed and accuracy
    C. run the gun yourself to avoid arguments
    D. have the experienced man run the gun and explain to the Inexperienced man that the next time the design department wants a quick check, it would be his turn at the transit

16. A Rockwell test is a test for

    A. water hardness
    B. well water purity
    C. hardness of metal
    D. rock bearing capacity

17. A slump test is made on a sample of concrete PRIMARILY to measure its

    A. finishing qualities
    B. resistance to bleeding
    C. strength
    D. workability

18. Of the following, the MOST important factor that the individual must fulfill in order to insure his own safety on a construction job is to

    A. be familiar with the specifications
    B. work slowly
    C. be alert
    D. wear clothing to suit the climatic condition

4 (#1)

19. Assume that a civil engineer is assigned as resident engineer on a minor construction contract.
Of the following statements relating to his assignment, the one that is CORRECT is:

   A. It is a good policy for the resident engineer to give orders directly to the contractor's men
   B. In checking for conformance with specifications, the resident engineer should rely on the word of the contractor rather than on the inspector's report
   C. The resident engineer generally should not interfere in matters of dispute between a contractor and his foreman
   D. It is permissible for the resident engineer to make a misrepresentation in order to obtain proof that the contractor failed to comply with the specifications

19.____

20. Of the following, the BEST method of dewatering a small deep hole in rock is to

   A. use well points to pump the area
   B. drive steel sheet piling and pump the area dry
   C. drive wood sheet piling and pump the area dry
   D. dig a sump in a low spot and pump the water from it

20.____

21. Batter piles are used in a pile foundation when

   A. the forces coming into the foundation are lateral
   B. obstructions in the soil merit their use
   C. the soil consists of material with a low-bearing capacity
   D. the elevation of the bedrock is too high to warrant the driving of normal piles

21.____

22. Of the following woods, the one that is NOT considered a hardwood is

   A. oak	B. maple	C. walnut	D. fir

22.____

23. The excavating unit which works BEST in soft-to-medium-hard materials, can dig holes extending far below the surface, and can lift the material to a high disposal point is the

   A. power shovel	B. clam shell
   C. orange peel	D. back-hoe

23.____

24. The PRIMARY reason for vibrating concrete is to

   A. force a maximum amount of water to the surface
   B. prevent segregation in the concrete
   C. move the concrete more easily into the forms
   D. prevent the formation of air pockets in the concrete

24.____

25. The rational method of estimating the rate of storm-water run-off is expressed by the formula Q = C i A.
In this formula,

   A. Q is the rate of run-off in cfs
   B. C is the coefficient of run-off in cfs
   C. i is the average intensity of precipitation in acre-inches
   D. A is the area in acre-inches

25.____

KEY (CORRECT ANSWERS)

1.	B	11.	C
2.	B	12.	C
3.	D	13.	A
4.	C	14.	C
5.	A	15.	B
6.	D	16.	C
7.	D	17.	D
8.	C	18.	C
9.	B	19.	C
10.	D	20.	D

21. A
22. D
23. B
24. D
25. A

TEST 2

DIRECTIONS: Each question or incomplete statement is followed by several suggested answers or completions. Select the one that BEST answers the question or completes the statement. *PRINT THE LETTER OF THE CORRECT ANSWER IN THE SPACE AT THE RIGHT.*

1. Of the following, the one which is NOT usually used for primary treatment of sewage is a   1.____
    A. comminutor B. grit chamber
    C. trickling filter D. skimming

2. Of the following, construction joints in reinforced concrete floor systems should be made at   2.____
    A. the edge of a beam
    B. the edge of a girder
    C. points of maximum shear
    D. points of maximum positive bending moment

3. To prevent objectionable deposits in a sanitary sewer, the MINIMUM average velocity when flowing full should be, in fps,   3.____
    A. 0.5 B. 1.2 C. 2.0 D. 3.0

4. The tool that is GENERALLY used in plaster work to float over freshly rodded brown mortar is   4.____
    A. darby B. featheredge C. paddle D. rod

5. An inferior paint well applied to a thoroughly cleaned and conditioned surface will give many times the protection and decorative effect that will be obtained by the best paint poorly applied to an uncleaned or damp surface.
Assuming that the above evaluation is correct, an APPROPRIATE instruction for your painting inspector, based on this statement, is   5.____
    A. to make sure that the paint used is equivalent to the approved sample
    B. to allow use of inferior paint provided the surface is clean and dry
    C. that the inspection of cleaning and painting of all surfaces is too casual
    D. to make sure the surface to be painted is clean and free from dampness

6. Of the following, the MOST compressible soil is usually   6.____
    A. sand B. clay C. gravel D. silt

7. Vitrified clay pipe   7.____
    A. can be ordered in lengths from 4 to 16 feet
    B. is easy to cut
    C. is joined by the use of Dresser Couplings
    D. is hard and brittle

8. A *hawk* is a tool USUALLY used in   8.____
    A. plastering B. brickwork
    C. roofing D. carpentry

2 (#2)

9. The specifications for concrete state that the water used for concrete shall be free of organic material.
   Of the following chemicals, the one that is organic is

   A. NaCl   B. $C_6H_{12}O_6$ C. HNO_3 D. $CaSO_4 2H_2O$

10. The *Proctor Test* is used in testing

    A. asphalt   B. concrete   C. soils   D. mortar

11. A rectangular reinforced concrete beam is to resist a bending moment of 75,000 pound-feet.
    If the effective depth is 20' and K $(= \frac{1}{2}f_c jk)$ is 180, the required width of the beam, in inches, is MOST NEARLY ($M=Kbd^2$)

    A. 12.3   B. 12.5   C. 12.7   D. 12.9

12. Of the following, the Chezy Formula, in reference to the flow of water, is used to compute the

    A. velocity   B. viscosity   C. pressure   D. losses

13. The length of a 20-penny nail is MOST NEARLY _____ inches.

    A. $2\frac{1}{2}$ B. 3   C. $3\frac{1}{2}$ D. 4

14. In the schedule of room finishes on an architectural plan of a building are the headings: Room, Space No., Floor, Base, Wall, Ceiling.
    The Base *most likely* refers to the

    A. wainscot
    B. material beneath the flooring material such as felt or paper
    C. material at the bottom of the wall
    D. structural material supporting the floor

15. Of the following, the STRONGEST and MOST DURABLE of all building stones used to face an exterior wall is

    A. trap   B. granite   C. limestone   D. sandstone

16. The width and thickness of the main plate of a riveted lap joint is 6" and 3/4", respectively. The allowable loads in shear, bearing, and tension are 70,000#, 80,000#, and 60,000#, respectively. The allowable f_s = 20000 psi.
    The efficiency of this joint is MOST NEARLY

    A. 82%   B. 55%   C. 75%   D. 66.7%

17. A post, consisting of a steel pipe whose net cross-sectional area is 40 sq. inches, is subjected to direct compression by a load of 80,000#.
    If the post is 8 ft. high, the reduction in length due to the load is, in inches, MOST NEARLY (E= 30,000,000#/sq. in. and $E = \frac{S}{E}$)

    A. .001   B. .006   C. .011   D. .016

18.

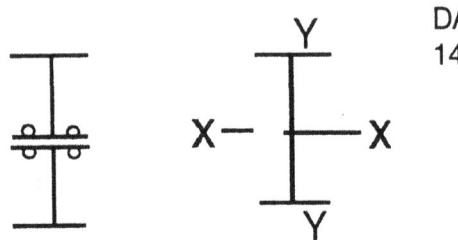

DATA:
14 WF 68 depth = 14 in.
width = 10 in.
area = 20 sq. in
I_{xx} = 724"4
I_{yy} = 121"4
r = $\sqrt{I/A}$

Two WF 68 columns are connected as shown above. Their LEAST radius of gyration when acting together as a unit is in inches, MOST NEARLY

A. 2.46 B. 4.92 C. 6.02 D. 12.04

19. The PRIMARY physical difference between steel and cast iron is that steel is much

A. *lighter* than cast iron
B. *weaker* in compression
C. *stronger* in tension
D. *weaker* in tension

20. Of the following, the one that is an example of a flexible pavement is a

A. gravel base and a concrete wearing course
B. plain concrete slab
C. gravel base and a bituminous wearing course
D. concrete base and an asphalt wearing course

21. Shutoff valves on 12" water supply lines found in the city streets USUALLY are _____ valves.

A. gate B. globe C. check D. stop

22. An analysis of drinking water shows that the pH is 6.0. The pH may be increased by adding

A. H_2SO_4
B. chlorine
C. caustic soda
D. fluorine

23.

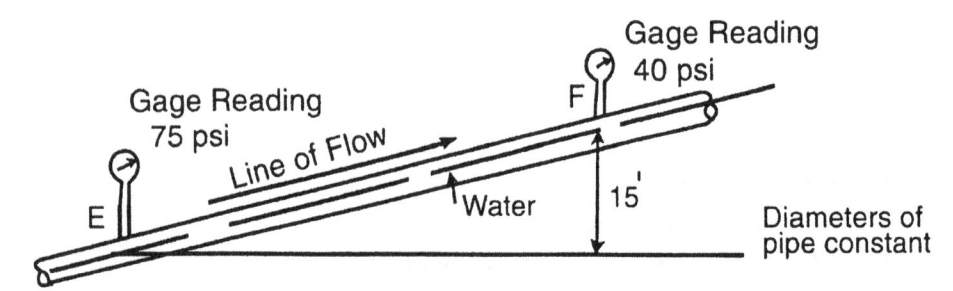

The head loss between E and F is, in feet of water, MOST NEARLY

A. 66 B. 81 C. 90 D. 93

24. A contract for a new building is generally broken into four separate contracts. These contracts are USUALLY: 24._____

    A. General Construction, Plumbing & Drainage, Heating and Ventilating, Electrical
    B. Foundation, Superstructure, Electrical, Mechanical
    C. Structural, Mechanical, Electrical, Foundation
    D. General Construction, Plumbing, Drainage, Electrical

25. The terms *shakes, checks, seasoning,* and *preservation* are all likely to be used in specifications for 25._____

    A. glass brick   B. cast iron
    C. plaster   D. timber

KEY (CORRECT ANSWERS)

1.	C	11.	B
2.	D	12.	A
3.	C	13.	D
4.	A	14.	C
5.	D	15.	B
6.	B	16.	D
7.	D	17.	B
8.	A	18.	A
9.	B	19.	C
10.	C	20.	C

21. A
22. C
23. A
24. A
25. D

EXAMINATION SECTION
TEST 1

DIRECTIONS: Each question or incomplete statement is followed by several suggested answers or completions. Select the one that BEST answers the question or completes the statement. *PRINT THE LETTER OF THE CORRECT ANSWER IN THE SPACE AT THE RIGHT.*

1. An unbalanced bid is a bidding device used by the contractor. An example of unbalanced bidding is to put

    A. lower unit prices in all unit price items to submit a low bid
    B. lower prices on lump sum items and higher prices on unit price items
    C. lower unit prices on secondary items and higher unit prices on primary items
    D. higher prices on items built early and lower prices on items built later

    1.____

2. Clearing and grubbing as related to excavation mean cutting trees

    A. so that 1 foot remains above ground
    B. so that 6 inches remains above ground
    C. to ground level
    D. and removing the stumps of the trees

    2.____

3. The size of a bulldozer is measured by its

    A. weight   B. flywheel horsepower
    C. ripping capacity   D. coefficient of traction

    3.____

4. Of the following, an important use of geotextiles is

    A. as a filter in drainage control
    B. to improve the density of soil
    C. to increase the plasticity of soil
    D. to reduce the CBR of soil

    4.____

5. A graphical procedure employing a control chart is sometimes used for statistical control in highway construction. After charts of individual tests are prepared, the upper and lower limits are usually _____ standard deviation(s) from a central value.

    A. one   B. two   C. three   D. four

    5.____

6. On a highway construction job, slope stakes are usually set on both sides of the road at intervals of _____ feet.

    A. 25   B. 50   C. 75   D. 100

    6.____

7. Earth grade stakes are usually set

    A. when the slope stakes are set
    B. at the center line of the road
    C. after final grading is completed
    D. after rough grading operations have been completed

    7.____

8. In a borrow pit, measurements for the volume of earth removed are taken usually at _____ foot intervals.

   A. 25   B. 50   C. 75   D. 100

9. In placing surveying stakes for a culvert, a stake is set at the center line of the culvert. A horizontal line on the stake gives the amount of cut or fill to the _____ of the culvert.

   A. top   B. center   C. flow line   D. subgrade

10. Aeolian soils are soils formed by

    A. glacial action
    B. volcanic action
    C. being carried by water
    D. being carried by wind

11. Specific gravity of soils are in the range of

    A. 2.3 to 2.5
    B. 2.4 to 2.6
    C. 2.5 to 2.7
    D. 2.6 to 2.8

12. Of the following soils, the one that is most highly compressible has a _____ plastic limit and _____ liquid limit.

    A. low; high
    B. low; low
    C. high; low
    D. high; high

13. In the present ASSHTO soil classification systems, soils are classified into groups. The number of basic groups are

    A. 6   B. 7   C. 8   D. 9

14. In the present AASHTO soil classification system, granular materials are primarily in Group(s)

    A. A1 only
    B. A1 and A2
    C. A1, A2, and A3
    D. A1, A2, A3, and A4

15. The optimum moisture content of a soil occurs when under a given compactive effort, the soil has a maximum

    A. void ratio
    B. plasticity index
    C. elasticity
    D. density

16. The liquid limit that separates an A4 soil from an A5 soil is

    A. 10   B. 20   C. 30   D. 40

17. As part of the soil classification in a given soil is an abbreviation NP. This is an abbreviation for no

    A. permeability
    B. plasticity
    C. peat or other organic materials
    D. porosity

18. For granular materials, the maximum allowable percent passing a Number 200 sieve is

    A. 20   B. 25   C. 30   D. 35

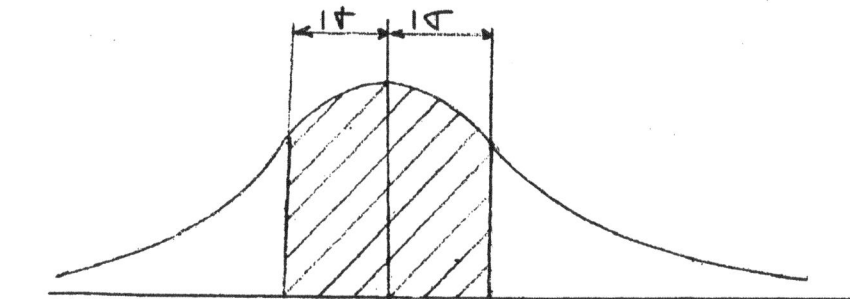

19. In the normal or Gauss distribution shown above, the shaded area is one standard deviation on either side of the central value covering _____ of the area under the curve.

   A. 60%   B. 62%   C. 65%   D. 68%

Questions 20-25.

DIRECTIONS: Questions 20 through 25, inclusive, refer to the diagram below of a vertical curve.

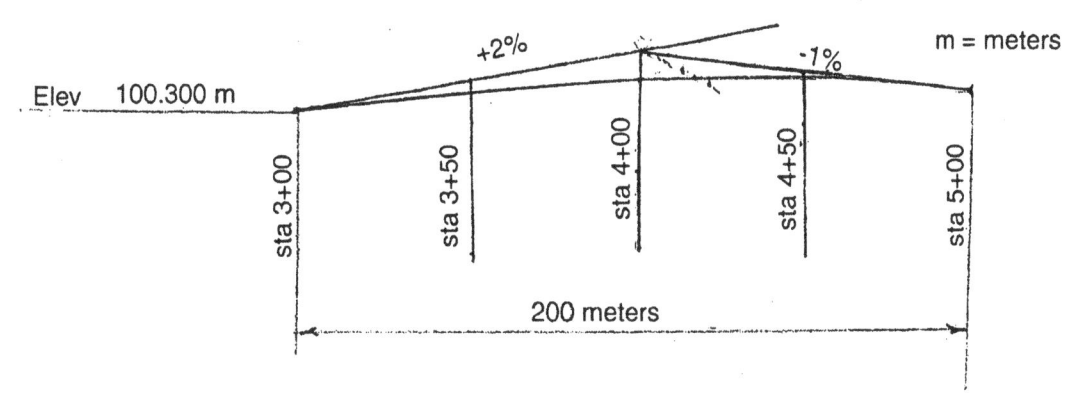

20. The elevation of the curve at Sta4+00 is _____ meters.

   A. 101.250   B. 101.350   C. 101.850   D. 102.150

21. The grade of the curve at Sta4+00 is

   A. +.5%   B. +.75%   C. +1.00%   D. +1.25%

22. The elevation of the curve at Sta3+50 is _____ meters.

   A. 100.992   B. 101.012   C. 101.112   D. 101.212

23. The grade of the curve at Sta3+50 is

   A. 1.75%   B. 1.50%   C. 1.38%   D. 1.25%

24. The station of the high point is

   A. 4+08.333   B. 4+16.667   C. 4+25.000   D. 4+33.333

25. The elevation of the high point is _____ meters.

   A. 101.633   B. 101.750   C. 101.833   D. 101.917

KEY (CORRECT ANSWERS)

1.	D	11.	D
2.	D	12.	A
3.	B	13.	B
4.	A	14.	C
5.	C	15.	D
6.	B	16.	D
7.	D	17.	B
8.	A	18.	D
9.	C	19.	D
10.	D	20.	B

21. A
22. C
23. D
24. D
25. A

TEST 2

DIRECTIONS: Each question or incomplete statement is followed by several suggested answers or completions. Select the one that BEST answers the question or completes the statement. *PRINT THE LETTER OF THE CORRECT ANSWER IN THE SPACE AT THE RIGHT.*

Questions 1-3.

DIRECTIONS: Questions 1 through 3 refer to the diagram below.

EI is constant

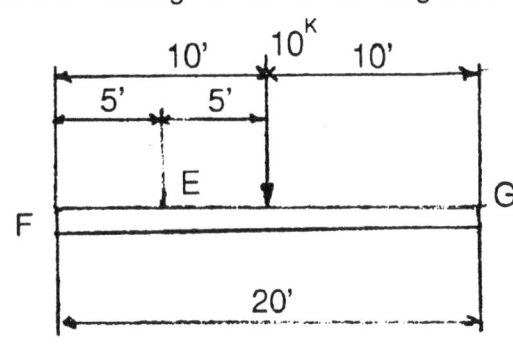

1. The deflection at the center of the beam is

   A. $-\dfrac{1670^{k13}}{EI}$ B. $-\dfrac{2000^{k13}}{EI}$ C. $-\dfrac{2330^{k13}}{EI}$ D. $-\dfrac{2670^{k13}}{EI}$

2. The slope at F is

   A. $-\dfrac{200^{k12}}{EI}$ B. $-\dfrac{225^{k12}}{EI}$ C. $-\dfrac{250^{k12}}{EI}$ D. $-\dfrac{275^{k12}}{EI}$

3. The deflection at E is

   A. $-\dfrac{966^{k13}}{EI}$ B. $-\dfrac{1046^{k13}}{EI}$ C. $-\dfrac{1096^{k13}}{EI}$ D. $-\dfrac{1146^{k13}}{EI}$

Questions 4-7.

DIRECTIONS: Questions 4 through 7, inclusive, refer to the truss below.

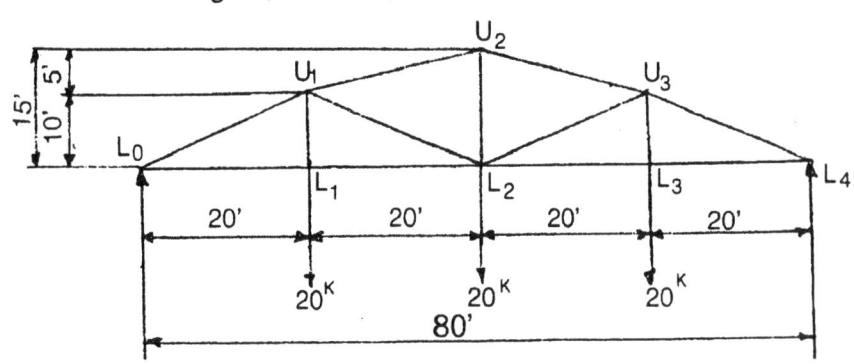

4. The load in member L_1-L_2 is

   A. $+30^k$ B. $+40^k$ C. $+50^k$ D. $+60^k$

5. The load in member U_1-U_2 is

   A. -50.9^k B. -52.9^k C. -54.9^k D. -56.9^k

6. The load in member U_1-L_2 is

   A. -3.4^k B. -5.4^k C. -7.4^k D. -9.4^k

7. The load in member U_2-L_2 is

   A. $+24.6^k$ B. $+26.6^k$ C. $+28.6^k$ D. $+30.6^k$

Questions 8-11.

DIRECTIONS: Questions 8 through 11, inclusive, refer to the diagram below of a beam with fixed ends.

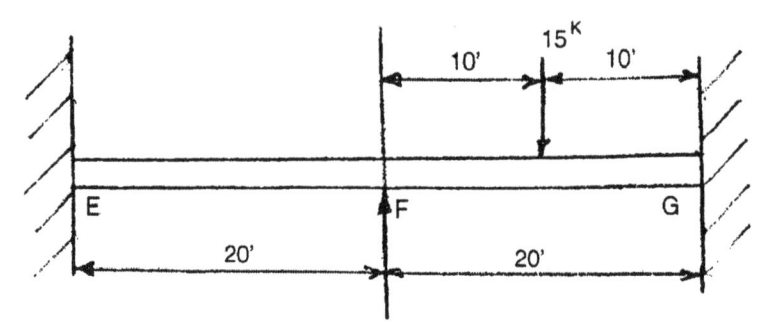

I is uniform

$$FEM = \frac{PL}{8}$$

8. The moment in E is

   A. 9.4^{lk} B. 12.6^{lk} C. 14.8^{lk} D. 17.0^{lk}

9. The moment in G is

   A. 37.5^{lk} B. 40.0^{lk} C. 43.0^{lk} D. 46.9^{lk}

10. The moment at F is

    A. 14.4^{lk} B. 18.8^{lk} C. 23.2^{lk} D. 27.6^{lk}

11. The vertical reaction at E is

    A. -0.4^k B. -1.4^k C. -2.4^k D. -3.4^k

12. The former First Lady of the United States who had legislation enacted to plant wild flowers adjacent to federal highways is

    A. Rosalyn Carter B. Barbara Bush
    C. Jackie Kennedy D. Lady Bird Johnson

13. *Scarification* as used in the specifications means

    A. removing rust from a surface
    B. removing paint from a surface
    C. cleaning equipment
    D. loosening topsoil

14. A proposal by the contractor producing a savings to the department without impairing essential functions and characteristics of the facility is termed a(n)

    A. alternative suggestion
    B. design efficiency proposal
    C. value engineering proposal
    D. force account economy

15. A cubic meter is MOST NEARLY equal to _____ cubic yards.

    A. 1.31   B. 1.33   C. 1.35   D. 1.37

16. One hectare is equal to MOST NEARLY _____ acres.

    A. 2   B. 2.5   C. 3.0   D. 3.5

17. One newton is MOST NEARLY equal to _____ pounds.

    A. .12   B. .17   C. .22   D. .29

18. A metric ton is _____ pounds.

    A. 2200   B. 2400   C. 2600   D. 2800

19. A piezometer is a device that measures

    A. hydraulic pressure   B. soil compaction
    C. soil grain size   D. soil grain strength

20. Portland cement type 2 is _____ cement.

    A. high early strength
    B. low heat
    C. air entraining
    D. moderate sulfate resisting

21. Wire shall have a minimum yield strength of 240 MPa. The MPa is an abbreviation of _____ pascals.

    A. macro   B. micro   C. milli   D. mega

22. 7°C is, in degrees Fahrenheit,

    A. 42.6   B. 44.6   C. 46.6   D. 48.6

23. In a concrete mix, the absolute ratio of the weight of water to the weight of cement is .44. If a bag of cement weighs 94 pounds and there are 7.48 gallons in a cubic foot, the number of gallons of water per bag of cement for this ratio is MOST NEARLY

    A. 5.0   B. 5.5   C. 5.8   D. 6.1

24. The specifications require that when transit mixed concrete is used, approximately 90% of the design water is added followed by mixing the concrete in the drum of the truck. The remainder of the design water may be added

    A. after half the load is emptied
    B. to meet the water cement ratio requirement
    C. if the mix is not uniform
    D. to attain a suitable slump

24.____

25. For highways, the minimum median width in a divided highway is _____ feet.

    A. 2   B. 3   C. 4   D. 5

25.____

KEY (CORRECT ANSWERS)

1. A	11. B
2. C	12. D
3. D	13. D
4. D	14. C
5. C	15. A
6. C	16. B
7. B	17. C
8. A	18. A
9. D	19. A
10. B	20. D

21. D
22. B
23. A
24. D
25. C

EXAMINATION SECTION
TEST 1

DIRECTIONS: Each question or incomplete statement is followed by several suggested answers or completions. Select the one that BEST answers the question or completes the statement. *PRINT THE LETTER OF THE CORRECT ANSWER IN THE SPACE AT THE RIGHT.*

1. Management by exception (MBE) is

    A. designed to locate bottlenecks
    B. designed to pinpoint superior performance
    C. a form of index locating
    D. a form of variance reporting

    1.____

2. In managerial terms, gap analysis is useful primarily in

    A. problem solving
    B. setting standards
    C. inventory control
    D. locating bottlenecks

    2.____

3. ABC analysis involves

    A. problem solving
    B. indexing
    C. brainstorming
    D. inventory control

    3.____

4. The Federal Discrimination in Employment Act as amended in 1978 prohibits job discrimination based on age for persons between the ages of

    A. 35 and 60   B. 40 and 65   C. 45 and 65   D. 40 and 70

    4.____

5. Inspectors should be familiar with the contractor's CPM charts for a construction job primarily to determine if

    A. the job is on schedule
    B. the contractor is using the charts correctly
    C. material is on hand to keep the job on schedule
    D. there is a potential source of delay

    5.____

6. The value engineering approach is frequently found in public works contracts. Value engineering is

    A. an effort to cut down or eliminate extra work payments
    B. a team approach to optimize the cost of the project
    C. to insure that material and equipment will perform as specified
    D. to insure that insurance costs on the project can be minimized

    6.____

7. Historically, most costly claims have been either for

    A. unreasonable inspection requirements or unforeseen weather conditions
    B. unreasonable specification requirements or unreasonable completion time for the contract
    C. added costs due to inflation or unavailability of material
    D. delays or alleged changed conditions

    7.____

8. A claim is a

   A. dispute that cannot be resolved
   B. dispute arising from ambiguity in the specifications
   C. dispute arising from the quality of the work
   D. recognition that the courts are the sole arbiters of a dispute

9. Disputes arising between a contractor and the owning agency are

   A. the result of inflexibility of either or both parties to the dispute
   B. mainly the result of shortcomings in the design
   C. the result of shortcomings in the specifications
   D. inevitable

Questions 10-13.

DIRECTIONS: Questions 10 through 13, inclusive, refers to the array of numbers listed below.

16, 7, 9, 5, 10, 8, 5, 1, 2

10. The mean of the numbers is

    A. 2   B. 5   C. 7   D. 8

11. The median of the numbers is

    A. 2   B. 5   C. 7   D. 8

12. The mode of the numbers is

    A. 2   B. 5   C. 7   D. 8

13. In statistical measurements, a subgroup that is representative of the entire group is a

    A. commutative group   B. sample
    C. central index   D. Abelian group

14. Productivity is the ratio of

    A. $\dfrac{\text{product costs}}{\text{labor costs}}$

    B. $\dfrac{\text{cost of final product}}{\text{cost of materials}}$

    C. $\dfrac{\text{outputs}}{\text{inputs}}$

    D. $\dfrac{\text{outputs cost}}{\text{time needed to product the output}}$

15. Downtime is the time a piece of equipment is

    A. idle waiting for other equipment to become available
    B. not being used for the purpose it was intended

C. being used inefficiently
D. unavailable for use

16. Index numbers

    A. relates to the cost of a product as material costs vary
    B. allows the user to find the variation from the norm
    C. are a way of comparing costs of different approaches to a problem
    D. a way of measuring and comparing changes over a period of time

17. The underlying idea behind Management by Objectives is to provide a mechanism for managers to

    A. coordinate personal and departmental plans with organizational goals
    B. motivate employees by having them participate in job decisions
    C. motivate employees by training them for the next higher position
    D. set objectives that are reasonable for the employees to attain, thus improving self-esteem among the employees

18. The ultimate objective of the project manager in planning and scheduling a project is to

    A. meet the completion dates of the project
    B. use the least amount of labor on the project
    C. use the least amount of material on the project
    D. prevent interference between the different trades

19. Scheduling with respect to the critical path method usually does not involve

    A. cost allocation
    B. starting and finishing time
    C. float for each activity
    D. project duration

20. When CPM is used on a construction project, updates are most commonly made

    A. weekly   B. every two weeks
    C. monthly   D. every two months

Questions 21-24.

DIRECTIONS: Questions 21 through 24 refer to the following network.

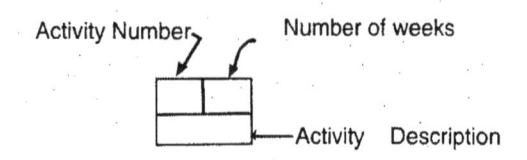

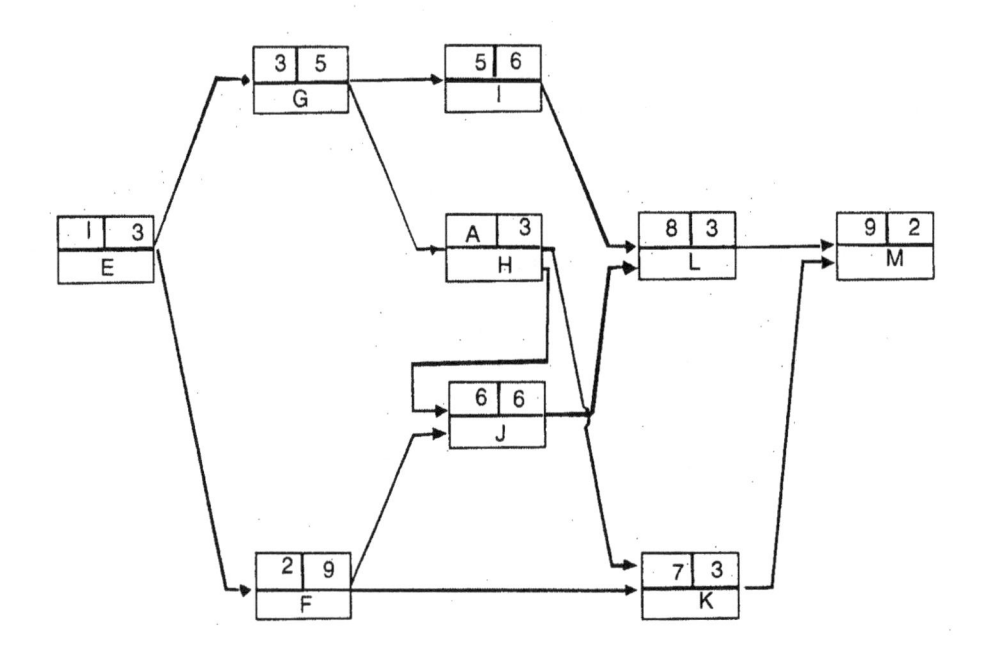

Activity Number	Activity Description	Duration in Weeks	Early Start	Early Finish	Late Start	Late Finish	Total Slack
1	E	3					
2	F	9					
3	G	5					
4	H	3					
5	I	6					
6	J	6					
7	K	3					
8	L	3					
9	M	2					

21. The critical path is

    A. E G H J L M   B. E G I L M
    C. E F J L M   D. E G H K M

21._____

22. The minimum time needed to complete the job is, in weeks,

    A. 19   B. 21   C. 22   D. 23

22._____

23. The slack time in J is, in weeks,

    A. 0   B. 1   C. 2   D. 3

23._____

24. The slack time in K is, in weeks,

    A. 4   B. 5   C. 6   D. 7

24._____

25. Of the following, the primary objective of CPM is to 25.____
    A. eliminate duplication of work
    B. overcome obstacles such as bad weather
    C. spot potential bottlenecks
    D. save on the cost of material

KEY (CORRECT ANSWERS)

1.	D	11.	C
2.	A	12.	B
3.	D	13.	B
4.	D	14.	C
5.	A	15.	D
6.	B	16.	D
7.	D	17.	A
8.	A	18.	A
9.	D	19.	A
10.	C	20.	C

21. C
22. D
23. A
24. C
25. C

TEST 2

DIRECTIONS: Each question or incomplete statement is followed by several suggested answers or completions. Select the one that BEST answers the question or completes the statement. *PRINT THE LETTER OF THE CORRECT ANSWER IN THE SPACE AT THE RIGHT.*

1. Gantt refers to
   - A. bar charts
   - B. milestone charts
   - C. PERT networks
   - D. Management by Objectives

   1.____

2. PERT is an abbreviation for

   - A. Progress Evaluation in Real Time
   - B. Preliminary Evaluation of Running Time
   - C. Program Evaluation Review Techniques
   - D. Program Estimation and Repair Times

   2.____

3. In project management terms, slack is equivalent to
   - A. tare
   - B. off time
   - C. delay
   - D. float

   3.____

4. The FIRST step in planning and programming a roadway pavement management system is to evaluate

   - A. priorities for the work to be done
   - B. the condition of your equipment
   - C. the condition of the roads in the system
   - D. the storage and maintenance facilities

   4.____

5. Managers accomplish their work in an ever changing environment by integrating three time-tested approaches. The one of the following that is NOT a time-tested approach is

   - A. scientific adaptation
   - B. scientific management
   - C. behavior management
   - D. management sciences

   5.____

6. The most effective managers manage for optimum results. This means that the manager is seeking to _____ a given situation.

   - A. get the maximum results from
   - B. get the most favorable results from
   - C. get the most reasonable results from
   - D. satisfy the conflicting interests in

   6.____

7. If a manager believes that an employee is irresponsible, the employee, in subtle response to the manager's assessment, will in fact prove to be irresponsible. This is an example of a(n)

   - A. conditioned reflex
   - B. self-fulfilling prophesy
   - C. Freudian response
   - D. automatic reaction

   7.____

8. Perhaps nothing distinguishes the younger generation from the older so much as the value placed on work. The older generation was generally raised to believe in the Protestant work ethic.
   This ethic holds primarily that

   8.____

A. people should try to get the highest salary possible
B. work should help people to advance
C. work should be well done if it is interesting
D. work is valuable in itself and the person who does it focuses on his work

9. The standard method currently in use in inspecting bituminous paving is to inspect each activity in detail as the paving work is being installed. In recent years some agencies use a different method of inspection known as a(n)

   A. as-built quality control method
   B. statistically controlled quality assurance method
   C. data based history of previous contracts of this type
   D. performance evaluation of the completed paving contract

10. Aggregates for use in bituminous pavements should be tested for grading,

    A. abrasion, soundness, and specific gravity
    B. type of rock, abrasion, and specific gravity
    C. abrasion, soundness, and deleterious material
    D. specific gravity, chemical composition of the aggregate, and deleterious material

11. Of the following, the one that is LEAST likely to be a test for asphalt is

    A. specific gravity   B. flashpoint
    C. viscosity   D. penetration

12. According to the AASHO, for bituminous pavements PSI is an abbreviation for _____ Index.

    A. Present Serviceability   B. Pavement Smoothness
    C. Pavement Serviceability   D. Present Smoothness

13. According to the AASHO, a bituminous pavement that is in extremely poor condition will have a PSI

    A. above 5.5   B. above 3.5
    C. below 3.5   D. below 1.5

14. The U.S. Federal Highway Administration defines asphalt maintenance as including work designed primarily for rejuvenation or protection of existing surfaces less than _____ inch minimum thickness.

    A. 1/4   B. 1/2   C. 3/4   D. 1

15. The maintenance phase of a highway management system includes the establishment of a program and schedule of work based largely on budget considerations, the actual operations of crack filling, patching, etc. and

    A. inspection of completed work
    B. planning of future operations
    C. upgrading existing pavements
    D. acquisition and processing of data

16. In a bituminous asphalt pavement, the progressive separation of aggregate particles in a pavement from the surface downward or from the edges inward is the definition of

   A. alligatoring
   B. raveling
   C. scaling
   D. disintegration

17. The bituminous pavement condition for the purpose of overlay design includes ride quality, structural capacity, skid resistance, and

   A. durability
   B. age of the pavement
   C. CBR value
   D. surface distress

18. An asphalt mix is being transferred from an asphalt truck to the hopper of the paving machine. Blue smoke rises from the material being emptied into the hopper of the paving machine.
   Your conclusion should be that

   A. this is normal and is to be expected
   B. the mix is overheated
   C. the mix is too cold
   D. the mix is being transferred too rapidly

19. Polished aggregate in an asphalt pavement are aggregate particles that have been rounded and polished smooth by traffic. This is a

   A. *good* condition as it allows a smooth ride
   B. *good* condition as it preserves tires
   C. *poor* condition as it promotes skidding
   D. *poor* condition as it tends to break the bond between the asphalt and the aggregate

20. A slippery asphalt surface requires a skid-resistant surfacing material. Of the following, the cover that would be most appropriate is a(n)

   A. asphalt tack coat
   B. fog seal
   C. layer of sand rolled into the asphalt surface
   D. asphalt emulsion slurry seal

21. The maximum size of aggregate in a hot mix asphalt concrete surfacing and bases allowed by the Federal Highway Administration Grading A is _____ inch(es).

   A. 3/4   B. 1   C. 1 1/4   D. 1 1/2

22. Wet sand weighs 132 pounds per cubic foot and contains 8% noisture. The dry weight of a cubic foot of sand is _____ pounds.

   A. 122.2   B. 122.0   C. 121.7   D. 121.4

23. A very light spray application of 551h emulsified asphalt diluted with water is used on existing pavement as a seal to riinimize raveling and to enrich the surface of a dried-out pavement is known as a(n)

   A. prime coat
   B. tack coat
   C. fog seal
   D. emulsion seal

24. 90 kilometers per hour is equivalent to _____ miles per hour. 24._____

    A. 49   B. 54   C. 59   D. 64

25. In a table of pavement distress manifestations is a column broadly titled *Density of Pavement Distress*. 25._____
    This is equivalent to _____ of the defects.

    A. average depth   B. average area
    C. extent of occurrence   D. seriousness

KEY (CORRECT ANSWERS)

1.	A	11.	A
2.	A	12.	A
3.	D	13.	D
4.	C	14.	C
5.	A	15.	D
6.	B	16.	B
7.	B	17.	D
8.	D	18.	B
9.	B	19.	C
10.	C	20.	D

21. D
22. A
23. C
24. B
25. C

EXAMINATION SECTION
TEST 1

DIRECTIONS: Each question or incomplete statement is followed by several suggested answers or completions. Select the one that BEST answers the question or completes the statement. *PRINT THE LETTER OF THE CORRECT ANSWER IN THE SPACE AT THE RIGHT.*

1. What is represented by the architectural symbol shown at the right?

    A. Stone concrete
    B. Cinder concrete
    C. Gravel
    D. Plaster

2. Poured installation of fiberglass or mineral wool insulation material will typically occur at a rate of _____ cubic feet per day.

    A. 20   B. 80   C. 120   D. 180

3. What is the MOST effective method for backfilling excavated material?

    A. Sheepfoot roller
    B. Bulldozer
    C. Shoveling
    D. Pneumatic tamper

4. Approximately how many square feet of unfinished plank flooring can be installed in an average work day?

    A. 50   B. 150   C. 225   D. 300

5. Studs for concrete basement forms are typically spaced _____ apart.

    A. 18 inches   B. 2 feet   C. 4 feet   D. 8 feet

6. Most construction stone is calculated and purchased by the

    A. square foot
    B. linear foot
    C. cubic yard
    D. ton

7. When earth backfill is replaced at a site, it is required to be compacted to within _____% of the original density.

    A. 65-75   B. 75-90   C. 85-95   D. 80-100

8. What type of brick masonry unit is represented by the drawing shown at the right?
    A. Norman
    B. Norwegian
    C. Corner
    D. Skippy

9. A laborer on a plain gable roof will typically install approximately _____ bundles of straight shingles in an average work day.

    A. 3-5   B. 6-9   C. 10-15   D. 17-20

10. What material is applied behind wall support mesh to reduce plaster waste?

    A. Mastic
    B. Gypsum board
    C. Chicken wire
    D. Asphalt-saturated felt

11. A _____ line is represented by the mechanical _____ symbol shown at the right.

    A. fuel oil
    B. vent
    C. cold water
    D. hot water

12. Approximately how many square feet of exterior surface can be prepared for paint or stain in one hour?

    A. 50   B. 100   C. 150   D. 250

13. What tool is used to rough level concrete when it is still plastic?

    A. Drum   B. Header   C. Float   D. Screed

14. Most stains that are applied to heavy timber can cover about _____ square feet per gallon.

    A. 100   B. 250   C. 350   D. 550

15. Which of the following is NOT one of the three standard methods for installing glazed tile?

    A. Furan resin grout
    B. Full mortar beds
    C. Organic adhesives
    D. Dry-set thin cement

16. Generally, the cost for a buildings's heating/air conditioning make up about _____% of the total construction cost.

    A. 1-3   B. 4-8   C. 5-10   D. 8-12

17. What is represented by the electrical symbol shown at the right?

    A. Lock or key switch
    B. Two-way switch
    C. Switch with duplex receptacle
    D. Triplex receptacle

18. Most structural lumber is considered *yard dry* at a MAXIMUM of about _____% moisture content.

    A. 5   B. 10   C. 20   D. 30

19. What is the term for a wood or metal edge applied to the wall and used as a guide to determine the depth of plaster?

    A. Rake   B. Float   C. Screed   D. Stud

20. Approximately how many single rolls of wall covering can be hung by one worker in a typical work day?

    A. 12   B. 20   C. 30   D. 45

21. What is represented by the architectural symbol shown at the right?   21.____

    A. Structural tile   B. Concrete block
    C. Fire brick   D. Brick

22. Approximately how many square feet of interior wall space can one painter, using a roller, cover in an hour?   22.____

    A. 25-50   B. 100   C. 175-200   D. 250

23. Cement plaster scratch coat for tile installation can typically be applied at a rate of _____ square yards per work day.   23.____

    A. 150   B. 300   C. 500   D. 750

24. MOST gas lines are made of   24.____

    A. black iron   B. copper
    C. galvanized steel   D. plastic

25. For most types of resilient flooring installation, approximately how many hours of labor will be required to install 100 square feet?   25.____

    A. 1/2   B. 1   C. 3   D. 4 1/2

KEY (CORRECT ANSWERS)

1.	C	11.	C
2.	A	12.	B
3.	B	13.	C
4.	B	14.	B
5.	C	15.	A
6.	D	16.	B
7.	C	17.	C
8.	A	18.	C
9.	C	19.	C
10.	D	20.	C

21. C
22. C
23. B
24. A
25. C

TEST 2

DIRECTIONS: Each question or incomplete statement is followed by several suggested answers or completions. Select the one that BEST answers the question or completes the Statement. *PRINT THE LETTER OF THE CORRECT ANSWER IN THE SPACE AT THE RIGHT.*

1. Approximately how much labor will be required for the testing of a single unit of installed water or sewer line?

   A. 30 minutes B. 1 hour
   C. 2 hours   D. 3 hours

   1.____

2. Concrete reinforcing bars are sized according to _____ inch increments.

   A. 1/16   B. 1/8   C. 1/4   D. 1/2

   2.____

3. Approximately how many square feet of 4 1/4" x 4 1/4" glazed wall tile, set in mortar, can be applied in an average work day?

   A. 60   B. 130   C. 175   D. 220

   3.____

4. In residential work, what type of estimate is MOST likely to be used to estimate the cost of excavation work?

   A. Quantity survey
   B. Lump-sum amount
   C. Cost-per-square-foot estimate
   D. Unit cost estimate

   4.____

5. What type of brick masonry unit is represented by the drawing shown at the right?
   A. Trough
   B. Economy
   C. King Norman
   D. Engineer

   5.____

6. Which of the following types of windows would be MOST expensive to install?

   A. Aluminum, single-hung vertical
   B. Wood, double-hung
   C. Steel, projected vent
   D. Aluminum, projected vent

   6.____

7. For estimating the labor cost of the installation of tile base and cap units, the typical tile labor time should be multiplied by

   A. 1/2   B. 2   C. 3   D. 4

   7.____

8. What is represented by the architectural symbol shown at the right?

   A. Plywood   B. Vertical paneling
   C. Brick   D. Rough lumber

   8.____

9. Approximately how long should it take a 2-person crew to install 100 linear feet of 4" x 6" girder?

   A. 30 minutes
   B. 1 hour
   C. 3 hours
   D. 1 work day

10. Each of the following is considered a fixed overhead cost EXCEPT

    A. office rent
    B. job site utilities
    C. assembly space
    D. stationery

11. How many square feet of solid plywood roof sheathing should two carpenters be able to install in a typical work day?

    A. 400 B. 800 C. 1,000 D. 1,400

12. What type of concrete masonry unit is represented by the drawing shown at the right?
    A. Floor
    B. Bull nose
    C. Trough
    D. Jamb

13. Which type of paving material will generally take LONGEST to install?

    A. Asphalt
    B. Gravel base course
    C. Concrete curb/gutter
    D. Concrete sidewalk

14. If a roof needs to be framed for locations such as dormers, hips, or valleys, an estimator should calculate a reduction in output of _____%.

    A. 5 B. 10 C. 20 D. 30

15. What is represented by the architectural symbol shown at the right?

    A. Stone concrete
    B. Cinder concrete
    C. Gravel
    D. Rock

16. Which of the following types of tile for resilient flooring would be MOST expensive?

    A. Pure vinyl
    B. Cork
    C. Vinyl asbestos
    D. Rubberized marbleized

17. Installation of tempered or insulated glass will cost approximately _____% more than the installation of 1/4" polished plate glass.

    A. 20 B. 50 C. 75 D. 100

18. Most concrete is considered to be completely cured after a period of

    A. 1 1/2 weeks B. 28 days C. 45 days D. 4 months

19. What type of window is hinged at the top so that it may be opened outward at the bottom?

    A. Storm B. Casement C. Sash D. Awning

20. What is the usual thickness, in inches, for the finish coat in MOST plastering projects?

    A. 1/16 B. 1/8 C. 1/4 D. 1/2

21. Due to the *swell factor* involved in excavation, 1 cubic yard of excavated sand or gravel may measure _____% more as waste or backfill.

    A. 10 B. 20 C. 30 D. 50

22. What is represented by the electrical symbol shown at the right?
    A. Blanked outlet
    B. Signal push button
    C. Special purpose outlet
    D. Gauge

23. What type of nails are typically used for installing rafters?

    A. 4d B. 8d C. 12d D. 16d

24. Most flat interior paint averages a coverage of about _____ square feet per gallon.

    A. 100-150 B. 200-250 C. 300-400 D. 450-550

25. Which of the following types of doors would be MOST expensive?

    A. Hollow core, birch-veneer face
    B. Solid core, walnut-faced
    C. Hollow core, hardboard-faced
    D. Solid core, birch-veneer face

KEY (CORRECT ANSWERS)

1.	C	11.	D
2.	B	12.	D
3.	A	13.	C
4.	D	14.	B
5.	D	15.	A
6.	B	16.	A
7.	B	17.	D
8.	D	18.	B
9.	C	19.	D
10.	B	20.	B

21. B
22. C
23. D
24. C
25. B

TEST 3

DIRECTIONS: Each question or incomplete statement is followed by several suggested answers or completions. Select the one that BEST answers the question or completes the statement. *PRINT THE LETTER OF THE CORRECT ANSWER IN THE SPACE AT THE RIGHT.*

1. Most tubs, toilets, sinks, and lavatories require an average of _____ hours labor for the installation of finish plumbing.   1.____
   A. 3   B. 5   C. 7   D. 9

2. What size is most wire used for ranges and other heavy-draw equipment?   2.____
   A. 2-4   B. 5-7   C. 8-10   D. 12-16

3. A 4-man crew using hand application will typically be able to apply _____ square yards of gypsum plaster in one work day.   3.____
   A. 35-40   B. 45-60   C. 75-80   D. 85-100

4. A _____ is represented by the mechanical symbol shown at the right.   4.____
   A. lock and shield valve
   B. strainer
   C. pressure reducing valve
   D. drain line

5. What type of drywall surface is used for ceramic tile installation?   5.____
   A. Plain manila paper
   B. Chemically-treated paper
   C. Aluminum foil
   D. Greenboard

6. Which of the following steps in a grading-quantity estimation would be performed LAST?   6.____
   A. Determine approximate finish grade
   B. Calculate difference between cut and fill
   C. Estimate elevation of grid corners from contours
   D. Average the elevation of each grid square

7. In order to give desired rigidity to a wall, the top plates must overlap AT LEAST _____ inches at each joint along the wall.   7.____
   A. 12   B. 24   C. 48   D. 60

8. The horizontal framing member above window and door openings is called the   8.____
   A. molding   B. footer   C. chord   D. lintel

9. Which of the following waterproofing materials is MOST expensive?   9.____
   A. 30-lb. asphalt paper with elastic adhesive
   B. Elastomeric waterproofing (1/32")
   C. Asphalt-coated protective board, installed in mastic
   D. Sprayed-on bituminous coating

10. If a site lawn is seeded, for how long will a contractor typically assume the responsibility for maintaining the lawn?   10.____
    A. 3 weeks   B. 1 month   C. 3 months   D. 6 months

11. What is represented by the architectural symbol shown at the right?

    A. Brick
    B. Vertical paneling
    C. Ceramic tile
    D. Concrete block

12. In an average work day, approximately how many square feet of brick (on sand bed) paving can be laid down?

    A. 80-100   B. 600   C. 1800   D. 3000-4000

13. In lumber take-off and ordering, costs are kept separate and calculated for each of the following specifications EXCEPT

    A. size   B. grade   C. length   D. species

14. The excavation of sand will require an angle of repose (slope) of 1 ft. vertical to _____ ft. horizontal.

    A. 3/4   B. 1   C. 1 1/2   D. 2

15. Concrete sidewalks are typically poured to a depth of _____ inches.

    A. 2   B. 4   C. 6   D. 8

16. What type of concrete masonry unit is represented by the drawing shown at the right?
    A. Stretcher
    B. Pier
    C. Jamb
    D. Beam

17. Each of the following is a factor in estimating the total cost according to a quantity survey EXCEPT

    A. quantity of each material
    B. square foot area of building
    C. cost of labor for each unit of material
    D. profit

18. Approximately how many hours will it take carpentry labor to install 100 square feet of wall space, without openings?

    A. 1   B. 3   C. 5   D. 7

19. Each of the following is included in a site plan EXCEPT

    A. size of property
    B. legal description
    C. number of external doors
    D. driveways

20. What is represented by the electrical symbol shown at the right? 20.____

    A. Street light and bracket
    B. Call system
    C. Wall bracket light fixture
    D. Sound system

21. Normally, horizontal reinforcements for masonry walls are spaced about _____ inches apart. 21.____

    A. 18   B. 36   C. 48   D. 60

22. Which of the following paving materials is generally LEAST expensive? 22.____

    A. Brick on sand bed   B. Random flagstone
    C. Asphalt   D. Concrete

23. What type of nails are typically used for installing shingles? 23.____

    A. 4d   B. 8d   C. 12d   D. 16d

24. A miter joint is cut at a _____ ° angle. 24.____

    A. 30   B. 45   C. 60   D. 90

25. Generally, ceiling joists must be braced if the distance between supports is greater than 25.____

    A. 18 inches   B. 24 inches   C. 4 feet   D. 8 feet

KEY (CORRECT ANSWERS)

1.	A	11.	B
2.	C	12.	A
3.	C	13.	C
4.	A	14.	D
5.	B	15.	B
6.	B	16.	B
7.	C	17.	B
8.	D	18.	B
9.	C	19.	C
10.	C	20.	A

21. C
22. C
23. A
24. B
25. D

EXAMINATION SECTION
TEST 1

DIRECTIONS: Each question or incomplete statement is followed by several suggested answers or completions. Select the one that BEST answers the question or completes the statement. *PRINT THE LETTER OF THE CORRECT ANSWER IN THE SPACE AT THE RIGHT.*

1. One of your men is doing a new job incorrectly.
   The BEST action for you to take is to

   A. criticize him in the presence of the other men
   B. criticize him in private
   C. bring him up on charges
   D. show him how to do it correctly

2. Of the following, the BEST reason why it is unacceptable policy for you to become too friendly with the men you supervise is that the men may

   A. try to take advantage of your friendship
   B. resent your familiarity
   C. wish to borrow money from you
   D. be transferred to another unit

3. Of the following, the attitude for you to have toward your men in order to accomplish your job BEST is to be

   A. harsh and uncompromising
   B. firm and fair
   C. easygoing and forgiving
   D. aloof and unsocial

4. A man in your gang complains that the work is dirty.
   Of the following, the BEST action for you to take is to

   A. give the man only the clean jobs
   B. tell the man that the dirt is part of the working conditions
   C. tell the man to quit if he does not like the working conditions
   D. bring the man up on charges

5. Although you estimate that you will need 4 men to do a certain job, you bring 6 men to do the job.
   This practice is considered by authorities to be

   A. *good,* since you will be sure to get the job done on time
   B. *good,* since some men may get sick on the job and may be unable to work
   C. *poor,* since men may stand around doing nothing
   D. *poor,* since the work will not be divided evenly

6. One of your men tends to *goof off* whenever he has the chance.
   Of the following, the BEST procedure to follow first with respect to this man is to

   A. have him transferred to another unit
   B. deduct the estimated wasted time from his time off
   C. give him the hardest jobs
   D. watch him closely

7. If four men work seven hours during the day, the number of man-hours of work done is

   A. 4 B. 7 C. 11 D. 28

8. You should check that you have all the equipment and material you need for the day before work is started. Of the following, the BEST reason for personally making this check is that

   A. the men under your supervision cannot be trusted
   B. the men are usually too busy to check the material and equipment
   C. it is your responsibility to see that everything is in order
   D. it is very difficult to get help for checking once you are in the field

9. One of your men is injured on the job.
   The FIRST thing you should do is to

   A. assist the injured man
   B. find out the circumstances of the accident
   C. call the office to notify your supervisor of the accident
   D. fill out the paperwork relating to the accident

10. When investigating a complaint by a home owner of sewage backing up in a house, you find that the house trap in the basement is blocked.
    Of the following, the PROPER action for you to take is to

    A. call in a plumber for the home owner
    B. clean out the house trap
    C. tell the home owner to call in a plumber
    D. disconnect the house trap from the piping, clean it out, and reinstall the trap

11. If it takes four men fourteen days to do a certain job, seven men, working at the same rate, should be able to do the same job in _____ days.

    A. 8 B. 7 C. 6 D. 5

12. The men you supervise suggest that work be started an hour earlier so that they can leave an hour earlier at the end of the day.
    Of the following, the BEST action for you to take is to

    A. ignore the request
    B. start work an hour earlier
    C. tell them you will forward their suggestion to your superior
    D. report the men for insubordination

13. One of the men under your supervision tells you he is ill and would like to leave the job.
    Of the following, the BEST action for you to take is to

    A. grant the request
    B. report the man for trying to goof off
    C. take the man personally to the department doctor
    D. tell the man he has to work the rest of the day or he will lose a day's pay

14. One of your men scheduled to arrive at 8 A.M. calls you at noon to inform you that he will not be in because of personal business.
    Of the following, the BEST action for you to take FIRST is to

    A. tell him to take it off sick leave
    B. call the office and ask for a replacement
    C. tell the man he should have called in on or about 8 A.M.
    D. tell him to charge the absence to lateness

15. Assume that you are in the field and have completed your work 2 hours before quitting time. The men spend the remaining 2 hours sitting in a restaurant.
    This practice is considered by authorities to be

    A. *good*, as the men put in a full day
    B. *good*, as make-work is a poor policy
    C. *poor*, because it creates a bad public image
    D. *poor*, as it disrupts the restaurant's business

16. As a foreman, you insist that all mechanical equipment you use be PROPERLY serviced and maintained by your men. This policy is

    A. *poor*, since you may be pressuring the men
    B. *poor*, since the men may not cooperate
    C. *good*, since it helps prevent breakdown in equipment which can cause work to stop
    D. *good*, since the equipment is serviced on the men's time so that you get more work out of the men

17. Assume that the men you supervise are cleaning out a catchbasin and uncover a gun.
    Of the following, the BEST action to take is to

    A. notify the police department of the discovery
    B. throw the gun away because it probably does not work
    C. keep the gun since you may be able to repair it
    D. dismantle the gun before disposing of it because it may be loaded

18. While your crew is working, a passer-by stops and asks you what they are doing.
    Of the following, the BEST action to take is to

    A. tell him to mind his own business
    B. briefly explain your operation
    C. tell him to write a letter to the sewer department
    D. ignore the man and call the police if he persists

19. Your men should be careful not to break manhole covers. Of the following, the BEST reason for taking this precaution is that

    A. the cost of the manhole cover will be taken out of your paycheck
    B. the manhole cover can't be replaced
    C. manhole covers cost money to replace
    D. broken manhole covers are difficult to get rid of

20. While on the job, you teach your duties to one of the laborers. 20._____
    This practice is considered by authorities to be

    A. *poor*, because it shows favoritism
    B. *poor*, because this laborer may undermine your authority
    C. *good*, because the laborer will then be able to pass a promotion examination
    D. *good*, because the laborer can replace you in an emergency

---

KEY (CORRECT ANSWERS)

1.	D	11.	A
2.	A	12.	C
3.	B	13.	A
4.	B	14.	C
5.	C	15.	C
6.	D	16.	C
7.	D	17.	A
8.	C	18.	B
9.	A	19.	C
10.	C	20.	D

TEST 2

DIRECTIONS: Each question or incomplete statement is followed by several suggested answers or completions. Select the one that BEST answers the question or completes the statement. *PRINT THE LETTER OF THE CORRECT ANSWER IN THE SPACE AT THE RIGHT.*

1. The BEST reason for you to advise your men to be alert at all times while working in the street is that

    A. working in the street could be dangerous
    B. they may see some criminal activity
    C. somebody from the main office may be observing your men
    D. they may create a bad public image if they are not always alert

    1._____

2. It is GOOD practice to complete a report on an accident as soon as possible after the accident occurs MAINLY because

    A. paperwork should be submitted to the office on the same day an accident occurs
    B. if you do not you may forget some of the necessary details
    C. this gives you more time to change the report if this should be necessary
    D. the department can then immediately prepare its defense

    2._____

3. Official directives state that you are to report immediately by telephone if a manhole cover or basin grate is missing.
   Of the following, the BEST reason for having this requirement is to

    A. permit the cover or grate to be ordered if it is not on hand
    B. be able to assess the responsibility for this condition
    C. prevent an accident
    D. enable the sanitation department to clean the street

    3._____

4. A complainant is a

    A. city agency that responds to a complaint
    B. person filing a complaint
    C. crew member that responds to a complaint
    D. lawyer who defends a client against a complaint

    4._____

5. In filling out an accident form, there is a section entitled *Accident Type.*
   Of the following, the one that is an accident type is

    A. struck by falling object
    B. operated without authority
    C. worked too slowly
    D. engaged in horseplay

    5._____

6. On an accident report, there is an item labeled *Nature of Injury.*
   Of the following, the one that belongs in this category is

    A. fracture   B. carelessness
    C. defective equipment   D. loose clothing

    6._____

7. Of the following, the LEAST serious of the defects filed in a sewer report is

    A. broken casting   B. missing casting
    C. noisy manhole cover   D. backed up sewer

    7._____

8. When signing a time sheet, the employee must sign his name and his number. The BEST of the following reasons for requiring his number in addition to his name is

   A. to be sure the employee has not entered the wrong time on the time sheet
   B. to make it easier to contact the employee
   C. his signature may be difficult to read
   D. the employee is paid based on his number which is fed into the IBM machine

9. One of the men in your unit states that he will take off the next day to attend his father-in-law's funeral and wants to know if he can change the absence to sick leave. Of the following, the BEST answer you can give him is that

   A. he can charge half the time to sick leave and half to annual leave
   B. the rules do not permit this to be done
   C. this can only be done if his father-in-law had lived with him
   D. sick leave can be used this way only if he had 10 years or more in service

10. In addition to the Department of Water Resources, the Environmental Protection Administration consists of the

    A. Board of Water Supply, the Department of Sanitation, and the Department of Air Resources
    B. Department of Sanitation, the Department of Municipal Services, and the Department of Air Resources
    C. Department of Sanitation and the Department of Municipal Services
    D. Department of Sanitation and the Department of Air Resources

11. The government calendar year starts on _____ 1.

    A. June   B. July   C. May   D. January

12. A truck leaves the garage at 9:26 A.M. and returns the same day at 3:43 P.M. The period of time that the truck was away from the garage is MOST NEARLY _____ hours _____ minutes.

    A. 5; 17   B. 5; 43   C. 6; 17   D. 6; 26

13. Of the following, the BEST method for a foreman to use to teach a man how to lift a manhole cover safely is to

    A. tell him how to do it
    B. make a sketch showing the correct method to use
    C. actually lift a cover with the man watching
    D. let the man try to lift the cover and correct any mistakes

14. Assume that one of the laborers you supervise is unable to read well and that you have advised him to go evenings to school to learn to read and write English.
    According to good supervisory practice, the advice is considered to be

    A. *poor,* because it is none of your business
    B. *poor,* because a laborer does not have to know how to read
    C. *good,* because he can then go on to get a high school diploma
    D. *good,* because he will be able to read signs and avoid danger on the job

15. Assume that a new piece of mechanical equipment is brought to the job.
Of the following, the BEST way for the men to learn the proper use of the equipment is to

   A. have a representative of the company that manufactures the equipment come to the job and demonstrate its use
   B. let the men try out the equipment and learn the operation of the equipment by using it
   C. let the men read the instruction manual carefully before trying out the equipment
   D. deliver a lecture to the men that have to use the equipment on the proper use of the equipment

16. Assume that you are training a group of men on the adjustment of a high–pressure relief valve.
Of the following, the FIRST topic you should discuss with the men is

   A. the conditions under which it is necessary to adjust the relief valve
   B. how to order parts for the relief valve
   C. how the springs in the relief valve work
   D. how to take apart the relief valve

17. Assume that a new man is assigned to your unit and you explain to him exactly what is expected of him.
This procedure is

   A. *poor,* because the new man will feel that you are threatening him
   B. *poor,* because this leaves the new man with no freedom to do the job as he feels best
   C. *good,* because then the new man can quit if he does not like the foreman
   D. *good,* because the new man will know what is required of him

18. A foreman explains to a man a way of doing a particular job and the man says he does not understand.
Of the following, the BEST action for the foreman to take is to

   A. repeat the explanation
   B. let the man remain ignorant
   C. transfer the man to another unit
   D. tell the man he may understand the procedure at a later time

19. A new piece of equipment is ordered and the men who will use it are trained in its use before the equipment arrives on the job.
This practice is

   A. *poor,* because the order may be cancelled and time wasted
   B. *poor,* because it takes longer to train men when the equipment is not present
   C. *good,* because it keeps the men busy when they do not have anything to do
   D. *good,* because the equipment can immediately be put to use

20. You observe a man using a piece of equipment incorrectly. Of the following, the BEST action for you to take is to

   A. have somebody else work with the equipment
   B. transfer the man to another unit
   C. bring the man up on charges
   D. show him how to use the equipment correctly

20.____

KEY (CORRECT ANSWERS)

1.	A	11.	D
2.	B	12.	C
3.	C	13.	C
4.	B	14.	D
5.	A	15.	A
6.	A	16.	A
7.	C	17.	D
8.	C	18.	A
9.	B	19.	D
10.	D	20.	D

PREPARING WRITTEN MATERIAL

EXAMINATION SECTION
TEST 1

DIRECTIONS: Each of Questions 1 through 5 consists of a sentence which may or may not be an example of good formal English usage.

Examine each sentence, considering grammar, punctuation, spelling, capitalization, and awkwardness. Then choose the correct statement about it from the four options below it.

If the English usage in the sentence given is better than any of the changes suggested in options B, C, or D, pick option A. (Do not pick an option that will change the meaning of the sentence.

1. I don't know who could possibly of broken it.

    A. This is an example of good formal English usage.
    B. The word "who" should be replaced by the word "whom."
    C. The word "of" should be replaced by the word "have."
    D. The word "broken" should be replaced by the word "broke."

2. Telephoning is easier than to write.

    A. This is an example of good formal English usage.
    B. The word "telephoning" should be spelled "telephoneing."
    C. The word "than" should be replaced by the word "then."
    D. The words "to write" should be replaced by the word "writing."

3. The two operators who have been assigned to these consoles are on vacation.

    A. This is an example of good formal English usage.
    B. A comma should be placed after the word "operators."
    C. The word "who" should be replaced by the word "whom."
    D. The word "are" should be replaced by the word "is."

4. You were suppose to teach me how to operate a plugboard.

    A. This is an example of good formal English usage.
    B. The word "were" should be replaced by the word "was."
    C. The word "suppose" should be replaced by the word "supposed."
    D. The word "teach" should be replaced by the word "learn."

5. If you had taken my advice; you would have spoken with him.

    A. This is an example of good formal English usage.
    B. The word "advice" should be spelled "advise."
    C. The words "had taken" should be replaced by the word "take."
    D. The semicolon should be changed to a comma.

2 (#1)

KEY (CORRECT ANSWERS)

1. C
2. D
3. A
4. C
5. D

———

TEST 2

DIRECTIONS: Select the correct answer.

1. The *one* of the following sentences which is *MOST* acceptable from the viewpoint of correct grammatical usage is:

    A. I do not know which action will have worser results.
    B. tie should of known better.
    C. Both the officer on the scene, and his immediate supervisor, is charged with the responsibility.
    D. An officer must have initiative because his supervisor will not always be available to answer questions.

    1.____

2. The *one* of the following sentences which is *MOST* acceptable from the viewpoint of correct grammatical usage is:

    A. Of all the officers available, the better one for the job will be picked.
    B. Strict orders were given to all the officers, except he.
    C. Study of the law will enable you to perform your duties more efficiently.
    D. It seems to me that you was wrong in failing to search the two men.

    2.____

3. The *one* of the following sentences which does *NOT* contain a misspelled word is:

    A. The duties you will perform are similiar to the duties of a patrolman.
    B. Officers must be constantly alert to sieze the initiative.
    C. Officers in this organization are not entitled to special privileges.
    D. Any changes in procedure will be announced publically.

    3.____

4. The *one* of the following sentences which does *NOT* contain a misspelled word is:

    A. It will be to your advantage to keep your firearm in good working condition.
    B. There are approximately fourty men on sick leave.
    C. Your first duty will be to pursuade the person to obey the law.
    D. Fires often begin in flameable material kept in lockers.

    4.____

5. The *one* of the following sentences which does *NOT* contain a misspelled word is:

    A. Officers are not required to perform technical maintainance.
    B. He violated the regulations on two occasions.
    C. Every employee will be held responable for errors.
    D. This was his nineth absence in a year.

    5.____

KEY (CORRECT ANSWERS)

1. D
2. C
3. C
4. A
5. B

TEST 3

DIRECTIONS: Select the correct answer.

1. You are answering a letter that was written on the letterhead of the ABC Company jind signed by James H. Wood, Treasurer. What is usually considered to be the correct salutation to use in your reply?

    A. Dear ABC Company:
    B. Dear Sirs:
    C. Dear Mr. Wood:
    D. Dear Mr. Treasurer:

2. Assume that one of your duties is to handle routine letters of inquiry from the public. The one of the following which is usually considered to be MOST desirable in replying to such a letter is a

    A. detailed answer handwritten on the original letter of inquiry
    B. phone call, since you can cover details more easily over the phone than in a letter
    C. short letter giving the specific information requested
    D. long letter discussing all possible aspects of the question raised

3. The *CHIEF* reason for dividing a letter into paragraphs is to

    A. make the message clear to the reader by starting a new paragraph for each new topic
    B. make a short letter occupy as much of the page as possible
    C. keep the reader's attention by providing a pause from time to time
    D. make the letter look neat and businesslike

4. Your superior has asked you to send an e-mail from your agency to a government agency in another city. He has written out the message and has indicated the name of the government agency.
When you dictate the message to your secretary, which of the following items that your superior has *NOT* mentioned must you be sure to *include*?

    A. Today's date
    B. The full address of the government agency
    C. A polite opening such as "Dear Sirs"
    D. A final sentence such as "We would appreciate hearing from your agency in reply as soon as is convenient for you"

5. The one of the following sentence which is grammatically preferable to the others is:

    A. Our engineers will go over your blueprints so that you may have no problems in construction.
    B. For a long time he had been arguing that we, not he, are to blame for the confusion.
    C. I worked on this automobile for two hours and still cannot find out what is wrong with it.
    D. Accustomed to all kinds of hardships, fatigue seldom bothers veteran policemen.

KEY (CORRECT ANSWERS)

1. C
2. C
3. A
4. B
5. A

TEST 4

DIRECTIONS: Select the correct answer.

1. Suppose that an applicant for a job as snow laborer presents a letter from a former employer stating: "John Smith has a pleasing manner and never got into an argument with his fellow employees. He was never late or absent." This letter

    A. indicates that with some training Smith will make a good snow gang boss
    B. presents no definite evidence of Smith's ability to do snow work
    C. proves definitely that Smith has never done any snow work before
    D. proves definitely that Smith will do better than average work as a snow laborer

2. Suppose you must write a letter to a local organization in your section refusing a request in connection with collection of their refuse.
You should *start* the letter by

    A. explaining in detail the consideration you gave the request
    B. praising the organization for its service to the community
    C. quoting the regulation which forbids granting the request
    D. stating your regret that the request cannot be granted

3. Suppose a citizen writes in for information as to whether or not he may sweep refuse into the gutter. A Sanitation officer answers as follows:
Dear Sir:
   No person is permitted to litter, sweep, throw or cast, or direct, suffer or permit any person under his control to litter, sweep, throw or cast any ashes, garbage, paper, dust, or other rubbish or refuse into any public street or place, vacant lot, air shaft, areaway, backyard or court.

   Very truly yours,
John Doe

   This letter is *poorly* written CHIEFLY because

    A. the opening is not indented
    B. the thought is not clear
    C. the tone is too formal and cold
    D. there are too many commas used

4. A section of a disciplinary report written by a Sanitation officer states: "It is requested that subject Sanitation man be advised that his future activities be directed towards reducing his recurrent tardiness else disciplinary action will be initiated which may result in summary discharge." This section of the report is *poorly* written MAINLY because

    A. at least one word is misspelled
    B. it is not simply expressed
    C. more than one idea is expressed
    D. the purpose is not stated

5. A section of a disciplinary report written by an officer states: "He comes in late. He takes too much time for lunch. He is lazy. I recommend his services be dispensed with."
   This section of the report is *poorly* written MAINLY because

   A. it ends with a preposition
   B. it is not well organized
   C. no supporting facts are stated
   D. the sentences are too simple

KEY (CORRECT ANSWERS)

1. B
2. D
3. C
4. B
5. C

PREPARING WRITTEN MATERIAL

PARAGRAPH REARRANGEMENT
COMMENTARY

The sentences which follow are in scrambled order. You are to rearrange them in proper order and indicate the letter choice containing the correct answer at the space at the right.

Each group of sentences in this section is actually a paragraph presented in scrambled order. Each sentence in the group has a place in that paragraph; no sentence is to be left out. You are to read each group of sentences and decide upon the best order in which to put the sentences so as to form as well-organized paragraph.

The questions in this section measure the ability to solve a problem when all the facts relevant to its solution are not given.

More specifically, certain positions of responsibility and authority require the employee to discover connections between events sometimes, apparently, unrelated. In order to do this, the employee will find it necessary to correctly infer that unspecified events have probably occurred or are likely to occur. This ability becomes especially important when action must be taken on incomplete information.

Accordingly, these questions require competitors to choose among several suggested alternatives, each of which presents a different sequential arrangement of the events. Competitors must choose the MOST logical of the suggested sequences.

In order to do so, they may be required to draw on general knowledge to infer missing concepts or events that are essential to sequencing the given events. Competitors should be careful to infer only what is essential to the sequence. The plausibility of the wrong alternatives will always require the inclusion of unlikely events or of additional chains of events which are NOT essential to sequencing the given events.

It's very important to remember that you are looking for the best of the four possible choices, and that the best choice of all may not even be one of the answers you're given to choose from.

There is no one right way to solve these problems. Many people have found it helpful to first write out the order of the sentences, as they would have arranged them, on their scrap paper before looking at the possible answers. If their optimum answer is there, this can save them some time. If it isn't, this method can still give insight into solving the problem. Others find it most helpful to just go through each of the possible choices, contrasting each as they go along. You should use whatever method feels comfortable, and works, for you.

While most of these types of questions are not that difficult, we've added a higher percentage of the difficult type, just to give you more practice. Usually there are only one or two questions on this section that contain such subtle distinctions that you're unable to answer confidently, and you then may find yourself stuck deciding between two possible choices, neither of which you're sure about.

EXAMINATION SECTION
TEST 1

DIRECTIONS: The following groups of sentences need to be arranged in an order that makes sense. Select the letter preceding the sequence that represents the BEST sentence order. *PRINT THE LETTER OF THE CORRECT ANSWER IN THE SPACE AT THE RIGHT.*

1.
   I. The keyboard was purposely designed to be a little awkward to slow typists down.
   II. The arrangement of letters on the keyboard of a typewriter was not designed for the convenience of the typist.
   III. Fortunately, no one is suggesting that a new keyboard be designed right away.
   IV. If one were, we would have to learn to type all over again.
   V. The reason was that the early machines were slower than the typists and would jam easily.

   A. I, III, IV, II, V
   B. II, V, I, IV, III
   C. V, I, II, III, IV
   D. II, I, V, III, IV

   1.____

2.
   I. The majority of the new service jobs are part-time or low-paying.
   II. According to the U.S. Bureau of Labor Statistics, jobs in the service sector constitute 72% of all jobs in this country.
   III. If more and more workers receive less and less money, who will buy the goods and services needed to keep the economy going?
   IV. The service sector is by far the fastest growing part of the United States economy.
   V. Some economists look upon this trend with great concern.

   A. II, IV, I, V, III
   B. II, III, IV, I, V
   C. V, IV, II, III, I
   D. III, I, II, IV, V

   2.____

3.
   I. They can also affect one's endurance.
   II. This can stabilize blood sugar levels, and ensure that the brain is receiving a steady, constant supply of glucose, so that one is *hitting on all cylinders* while taking the test.
   III. By food, we mean real food, not junk food or unhealthy snacks.
   IV. For this reason, it is important not to skip a meal, and to bring food with you to the exam.
   V. One's blood sugar levels can affect how clearly one is able to think and concentrate during an exam.

   A. V, IV, II, III, I
   B. V, II, I, IV, III
   C. V, I, IV, III, II
   D. V, IV, I, III, II

   3.____

4.
   I. Those who are the embodiment of desire are absorbed in material quests, and those who are the embodiment of feeling are warriors who value power more than possession.
   II. These qualities are in everyone, but in different degrees.
   III. But those who value understanding yearn not for goods or victory, but for knowledge.
   IV. According to Plato, human behavior flows from three main sources: desire, emotion, and knowledge,

   4.____

V. In the perfect state, the industrial forces would produce but not rule, the military would protect but not rule, and the forces of knowledge, the philosopher kings, would reign.

A. IV, V, I, II, III
B. V, I, II, III, IV
C. IV, III, II, I, V
D. IV, II, I, III, V

5. I. Of the more than 26,000 tons of garbage produced daily in New York City, 12,000 tons arrive daily at Fresh Kills.
    II. In a month, enough garbage accumulates there to fill the Empire State Building.
    III. In 1937, the Supreme Court halted the practice of dumping the trash of New York City into the sea.
    IV. Although the garbage is compacted, in a few years the mounds of garbage at Fresh Kills will be the highest points south of Maine's Mount Desert Island on the Eastern Seaboard.
    V. Instead, tugboats now pull barges of much of the trash to Staten Island and the largest landfill in the world, Fresh Kills.

    A. III, V, IV, I, II
    B. III, V, II, IV, I
    C. III, V, I, II, IV
    D. III, II, V, IV, I

6. I. Communists rank equality very high, but freedom very low.
    II. Unlike communists, conservatives place a high value on freedom and a very low value on equality.
    III. A recent study demonstrated that one way to classify people's political beliefs is to look at the importance placed on two words: freedom and equality.
    IV. Thus, by demonstrating how members of these groups feel about the two words, the study has proved to be useful for political analysts in several European countries.
    V. According to the study, socialists and liberals rank both freedom and equality very high, while fascists rate both very low.

    A. III, V, I, II, IV
    B. III, IV, V, I, II
    C. III, V, IV, II, I
    D. III, I, II, IV, V

7. I. "Can there be anything more amazing than this?"
    II. If the riddle is successfully answered, his dead brothers will be brought back to life.
    III. "Even though man sees those around him dying every day," says Dharmaraj, "he still believes and acts as if he were immortal."
    IV. "What is the cause of ceaseless wonder?" asks the Lord of the Lake.
    V. In the ancient epic, <u>The Mahabharata,</u> a riddle is asked of one of the Pandava brothers.

    A. V, II, I, IV, III
    B. V, IV, III, I, II
    C. V, II, IV, III, I
    D. V, II, IV, I, III

8. I. On the contrary, the two main theories — the cooperative (neoclassical) theory and the radical (labor theory) — clearly rest on very different assumptions, which have very different ethical overtones.
    II. The distribution of income is the primary factor in determining the relative levels of material well-being that different groups or individuals attain.
    III. Of all issues in economics, the distribution of income is one of the most controversial.
    IV. The neoclassical theory tends to support the existing income distribution (or minor changes), while the labor theory tends to support substantial changes in the way income is distributed.
    V. The intensity of the controversy reflects the fact that different economic theories are not purely neutral, *detached* theories with no ethical or moral implications.

    A. II, I, V, IV, III
    B. III, II, V, I, IV
    C. III, V, II, I, IV
    D. III, V, IV, I, II

8.____

9. I. The pool acts as a broker and ensures that the cheapest power gets used first.
    II. Every six seconds, the pool's computer monitors all of the generating stations in the state and decides which to ask for more power and which to cut back.
    III. The buying and selling of electrical power is handled by the New York Power Pool in Guilderland, New York.
    IV. This is to the advantage of both the buying and selling utilities.
    V. The pool began operation in 1970, and consists of the state's eight electric utilities.

    A. V, I, II, III, IV
    B. IV, II, I, III, V
    C. III, V, I, IV, II
    D. V, III, IV, II, I

9.____

10. I. Modern English is much simpler grammatically than Old English.
    II. Finnish grammar is very complicated; there are some fifteen cases, for example.
    III. Chinese, a very old language, may seem to be the exception, but it is the great number of characters/ words that must be mastered that makes it so difficult to learn, not its grammar.
    IV. The newest literary language — that is, written as well as spoken — is Finnish, whose literary roots go back only to about the middle of the nineteenth century.
    V. Contrary to popular belief, the longer a language is been in use the simpler its grammar — not the reverse.

    A. IV, I, II, III, V
    B. V, I, IV, II, III
    C. I, II, IV, III, V
    D. IV, II, III, I, V

10.____

KEY (CORRECT ANSWERS)

1. D
2. A
3. C
4. D
5. C

6. A
7. C
8. B
9. C
10. B

TEST 2

DIRECTIONS: This type of question tests your ability to recognize accurate paraphrasing, well-constructed paragraphs, and appropriate style and tone. It is important that the answer you select contains only the facts or concepts given in the original sentences. It is also important that you be aware of incomplete sentences, inappropriate transitions, unsupported opinions, incorrect usage, and illogical sentence order. Paragraphs that do not include all the necessary facts and concepts, that distort them, or that add new ones are not considered correct.

The format for this section may vary. Sometimes, long paragraphs are given, and emphasis is placed on style and organization. Our first five questions are of this type. Other times, the paragraphs are shorter, and there is less emphasis on style and more emphasis on accurate representation of information. Our second group of five questions are of this nature.

For each of Questions 1 through 10, select the paragraph that BEST expresses the ideas contained in the sentences above it. *PRINT THE LETTER OF THE CORRECT ANSWER IN THE SPACE AT THE RIGHT.*

1. I. Listening skills are very important for managers.
    II. Listening skills are not usually emphasized.
    III. Whenever managers are depicted in books, manuals or the media, they are always talking, never listening.
    IV. We'd like you to read the enclosed handout on listening skills and to try to consciously apply them this week.
    V. We guarantee they will improve the quality of your interactions.

    A. Unfortunately, listening skills are not usually emphasized for managers. Managers are always depicted as talking, never listening. We'd like you to read the enclosed handout on listening skills. Please try to apply these principles this week. If you do, we guarantee they will improve the quality of your interactions.
    B. The enclosed handout on listening skills will be important improving the quality of your interactions. We guarantee it. All you have to do is take some time this week to read it and to consciously try to apply the principles. Listening skills are very important for managers, but they are not usually emphasized. Whenever managers are depicted in books, manuals or the media, they are always talking, never listening.
    C. Listening well is one of the most important skills a manager can have, yet it's not usually given much attention. Think about any representation of managers in books, manuals, or in the media that you may have seen. They're always talking, never listening. We'd like you to read the enclosed handout on listening skills and consciously try to apply them the rest of the week. We guarantee you will see a difference in the quality of your interactions.
    D. Effective listening, one very important tool in the effective manager's arsenal, is usually not emphasized enough. The usual depiction of managers in books, manuals or the media is one in which they are always talking, never listening. We'd like you to read the enclosed handout and consciously try to apply the information contained therein throughout the rest of the week. We feel sure that you will see a marked difference in the quality of your interactions.

1.____

2. I. Chekhov wrote three dramatic masterpieces which share certain themes and formats: Uncle Vanya, The Cherry Orchard, and The Three Sisters.
   II. They are primarily concerned with the passage of time and how this erodes human aspirations.
   III. The plays are haunted by the ghosts of the wasted life.
   IV. The characters are concerned with life's lesser problems; however, such as the inability to make decisions, loyalty to the wrong cause, and the inability to be clear.
   V. This results in a sweet, almost aching, type of a sadness referred to as Chekhovian.

   A. Chekhov wrote three dramatic masterpieces: Uncle Vanya, The Cherry Orchard, and The Three Sisters. These masterpieces share certain themes and formats: the passage of time, how time erodes human aspirations, and the ghosts of wasted life. Each masterpiece is characterized by a sweet, almost aching, type of sadness that has become known as Chekhovian. The sweetness of this sadness hinges on the fact that it is not the great tragedies of life which are destroying these characters, but their minor flaws: indecisiveness, misplaced loyalty, unclarity.
   B. The Cherry Orchard, Uncle Vanya, and The Three Sisters are three dramatic masterpieces written by Chekhov that use similar formats to explore a common theme. Each is primarily concerned with the way that passing time wears down human aspirations, and each is haunted by the ghosts of the wasted life. The characters are shown struggling futilely with the lesser problems of life: indecisiveness, loyalty to the wrong cause, and the inability to be clear. These struggles create a mood of sweet, almost aching, sadness that has become known as Chekhovian.
   C. Chekhov's dramatic masterpieces are, along with The Cherry Orchard, Uncle Vanya, and The Three Sisters. These plays share certain thematic and formal similarities. They are concerned most of all with the passage of time and the way in which time erodes human aspirations. Each play is haunted by the specter of the wasted life. Chekhov's characters are caught, however, by life's lesser snares: indecisiveness, loyalty to the wrong cause, and unclarity. The characteristic mood is a sweet, almost aching type of sadness that has come to be known as Chekhovian.
   D. A Chekhovian mood is characterized by sweet, almost aching, sadness. The term comes from three dramatic tragedies by Chekhov which revolve around the sadness of a wasted life. The three masterpieces (Uncle Vanya, The Three Sisters, and The Cherry Orchard) share the same theme and format. The plays are concerned with how the passage of time erodes human aspirations. They are peopled with characters who are struggling with life's lesser problems. These are people who are indecisive, loyal to the wrong causes, or are unable to make themselves clear.

3. I. Movie previews have often helped producers decide what parts of movies they should take out or leave in.
    II. The first 1933 preview of King Kong was very helpful to the producers because many people ran screaming from the theater and would not return when four men first attacked by Kong were eaten by giant spiders.
    III. The 1950 premiere of Sunset Boulevard resulted in the filming of an entirely new beginning, and a delay of six months in the film's release.
    IV. In the original opening scene, William Holden was in a morgue talking with thirty-six other "corpses" about the ways some of them had died.
    V. When he began to tell them of his life with Gloria Swanson, the audience found this hilarious, instead of taking the scene seriously.

3. _____

  A. Movie previews have often helped producers decide what parts of movies they should leave in or take out. For example, the first preview of King Kong in 1933 was very helpful. In one scene, four men were first attacked by Kong and then eaten by giant spiders. Many members of the audience ran screaming from the theater and would not return. The premiere of the 1950 film Sunset Boulevard was also very helpful. In the original opening scene, William Holden was in a morgue with thirty-six other "corpses," discussing the ways some of them had died. When he began to tell them of his life with Gloria Swanson, the audience found this hilarious. They were supposed to take the scene seriously. The result was a delay of six months in the release of the film while a new beginning was added.

  B. Movie previews have often helped producers decide whether they should change various parts of a movie. After the 1933 preview of King Kong, a scene in which four men who had been attacked by Kong were eaten by giant spiders was taken out as many people ran screaming from the theater and would not return. The 1950 premiere of Sunset Boulevard also led to some changes. In the original opening scene, William Holden was in a morgue talking with thirty-six other "corpses" about the ways some of them had died. When he began to tell them of his life with Gloria Swanson, the audience found this hilarious, instead of taking the scene seriously.

  C. What do Sunset Boulevard and King Kong have in common? Both show the value of using movie previews to test audience reaction. The first 1933 preview of King Kong showed that a scene showing four men being eaten by giant spiders after having been attacked by Kong was too frightening for many people. They ran screaming from the theater and couldn't be coaxed back. The 1950 premiere of Sunset Boulevard was also a scream, but not the kind the producers intended. The movie opens with William Holden lying in a morgue discussing the ways they had died with thirty-six other "corpses." When he began to tell them of his life with Gloria Swanson, the audience couldn't take him seriously. Their laughter caused a six-month delay while the beginning was rewritten.

  D. Producers very often use movie previews to decide if changes are needed. The premiere of Sunset Boulevard in 1950 led to a new beginning and a six-month delay in film release. At the beginning, William Holden and thirty-six other "corpses" discuss the ways some of them died. Rather than taking this seriously, the audience thought it was hilarious when he began to tell them of his life with Gloria Swanson. The first 1933 preview of King Kong was very helpful for its producers because one scene so terrified the audience that many of them ran screaming from the theater and would not return. In this particular scene, four men who had first been attacked by Kong were being eaten by giant spiders.

4. I. It is common for supervisors to view employees as "things" to be manipulated.   4.____
   II. This approach does not motivate employees, nor does the carrot-and-stick approach because employees often recognize these behaviors and resent them.
   III. Supervisors can change these behaviors by using self-inquiry and persistence.
   IV. The best managers genuinely respect those they work with, are supportive and helpful, and are interested in working as a team with those they supervise.
   V. They disagree with the Golden Rule that says "he or she who has the gold makes the rules."

   A. Some managers act as if they think the Golden Rule means "he or she who has the gold makes the rules." They show disrespect to employees by seeing them as "things" to be manipulated. Obviously, this approach does not motivate employees any more than the carrot-and-stick approach motivates them. The employees are smart enough to spot these behaviors and resent them. On the other hand, the managers genuinely respect those they work with, are supportive and helpful, and are interested in working as a team. Self-inquiry and persistence can change even the former type of supervisor into the latter.
   B. Many supervisors fall into the trap of viewing employees as "things" to be manipulated, or try to motivate them by using a carrot-and-stick approach. These methods do not motivate employees, who often recognize the behaviors and resent them. Supervisors can change these behaviors, however, by using self-inquiry and persistence. The best managers are supportive and helpful, and have genuine respect for those with whom they work. They are interested in working as a team with those they supervise. To them, the Golden Rule is not "he or she who has the gold makes the rules."
   C. Some supervisors see employees as "things" to be used or manipulated using a carrot-and-stick technique. These methods don't work. Employees often see through them and resent them. A supervisor who wants to change may do so. The techniques of self-inquiry and persistence can be used to turn him or her into the type of supervisor who doesn't think the Golden Rule is "he or she who has the gold makes the rules." They may become like the best managers who treat those with whom they work with respect and give them help and support. These are the managers who know how to build a team.
   D. Unfortunately, many supervisors act as if their employees are objects whose movements they can position at will. This mistaken belief has the same result as another popular motivational technique—the carrot-and-stick approach. Both attitudes can lead to the same result — resentment from those employees who recognize the behaviors for what they are. Supervisors who recognize these behaviors can change through the use of persistence and the use of self-inquiry. It's important to remember that the best managers respect their employees. They readily give necessary help and support and are interested in working as a team with those they supervise. To these managers, the Golden Rule is not "he or she who has the gold makes the rules."

5.
I. The first half of the nineteenth century produced a group of pessimistic poets — Byron, De Musset, Heine, Pushkin, and Leopardi.
II. It also produced a group of pessimistic composers—Schubert, Chopin, Schumann, and even the later Beethoven.
III. Above all, in philosophy, there was the profoundly pessimistic philosopher, Schopenhauer.
IV. The Revolution was dead, the Bourbons were restored, the feudal barons were reclaiming their land, and progress everywhere was being suppressed, as the great age was over.
V. "I thank God," said Goethe, "that I am not young in so thoroughly finished a world."

5.____

A. "I thank God," said Goethe, "that I am not young in so thoroughly finished a world." The Revolution was dead, the Bourbons were restored, the feudal barons were reclaiming their land, and progress everywhere was being suppressed. The first half of the nineteenth century produced a group of pessimistic poets: Byron, De Musset, Heine, Pushkin, and Leopardi. It also produced pessimistic composers: Schubert, Chopin, Schumann. Although Beethoven came later, he fits into this group, too. Finally and above all, it also produced a profoundly pessimistic philosopher, Schopenhauer. The great age was over.

B. The first half of the nineteenth century produced a group of pessimistic poets: Byron, De Musset, Heine, Pushkin, and Leopardi. It produced a group of pessimistic composers: Schubert, Chopin, Schumann, and even the later Beethoven. Above all, it produced a profoundly pessimistic philosopher, Schopenhauer. For each of these men, the great age was over. The Revolution was dead, and the Bourbons were restored. The feudal barons were reclaiming their land, and progress everywhere was being suppressed.

C. The great age was over. The Revolution was dead—the Bourbons were restored, and the feudal barons were reclaiming their land. Progress everywhere was being suppressed. Out of this climate came a profound pessimism. Poets, like Byron, De Musset, Heine, Pushkin, and Leopardi; composers, like Schubert, Chopin, Schumann, and even the later Beethoven; and, above all, a profoundly pessimistic philosopher, Schopenauer. This pessimism which arose in the first half of the nineteenth century is illustrated by these words of Goethe, "I thank God that I am not young in so thoroughly finished a world."

D. The first half of the nineteenth century produced a group of pessimistic poets, Byron, De Musset, Heine, Pushkin, and Leopardi — and a group of pessimistic composers, Schubert, Chopin, Schumann, and the later Beethoven. Above all, it produced a profoundly pessimistic philosopher, Schopenhauer. The great age was over. The Revolution was dead, the Bourbons were restored, the feudal barons were reclaiming their land, and progress everywhere was being suppressed. "I thank God," said Goethe, "that I am not young in so thoroughly finished a world."

6.
I. A new manager sometimes may feel insecure about his or her competence in the new position.
II. The new manager may then exhibit defensive or arrogant behavior towards those one supervises, or the new manager may direct overly flattering behavior toward one's new supervisor.

6.____

A. Sometimes, a new manager may feel insecure about his or her ability to perform well in this new position. The insecurity may lead him or her to treat others differently. He or she may display arrogant or defensive behavior towards those he or she supervises, or be overly flattering to his or her new supervisor.
B. A new manager may sometimes feel insecure about his or her ability to perform well in the new position. He or she may then become arrogant, defensive, or overly flattering towards those he or she works with.
C. There are times when a new manager may be insecure about how well he or she can perform in the new job. The new manager may also behave defensive or act in an arrogant way towards those he or she supervises, or overly flatter his or her boss.
D. Sometimes, a new manager may feel insecure about his or her ability to perform well in the new position. He or she may then display arrogant or defensive behavior towards those they supervise, or become overly flattering towards their supervisors.

7. I. It is possible to eliminate unwanted behavior by bringing it under stimulus control — tying the behavior to a cue, and then never, or rarely, giving the cue.
    II. One trainer successfully used this method to keep an energetic young porpoise from coming out of her tank whenever she felt like it, which was potentially dangerous.
    III. Her trainer taught her to do it for a reward, in response to a hand signal, and then rarely gave the signal.

7.____

A. Unwanted behavior can be eliminated by tying the behavior to a cue, and then never, or rarely, giving the cue. This is called stimulus control. One trainer was able to use this method to keep an energetic young porpoise from coming out of her tank by teaching her to come out for a reward in response to a hand signal, and then rarely giving the signal.
B. Stimulus control can be used to eliminate unwanted behavior. In this method, behavior is tied to a cue, and then the cue is rarely, if ever, given. One trainer was able to successfully use stimulus control to keep an energetic young porpoise from coming out of her tank whenever she felt like it — a potentially dangerous practice. She taught the porpoise to come out for a reward when she gave a hand signal, and then rarely gave the signal.
C. It is possible to eliminate behavior that is undesirable by bringing it under stimulus control by tying behavior to a signal, and then rarely giving the signal. One trainer successfully used this method to keep an energetic young porpoise from coming out of her tank, a potentially dangerous situation. Her trainer taught the porpoise to do it for a reward, in response to a hand signal, and then would rarely give the signal.
D. By using stimulus control, it is possible to eliminate unwanted behavior by tying the behavior to a cue, and then rarely or never give the cue. One trainer was able to use this method to successfully stop a young porpoise from coming out of her tank whenever she felt like it. To curb this potentially dangerous practice, the porpoise was taught by the trainer to come out of the tank for a reward, in response to a hand signal, and then rarely given the signal.

8. I. There is a great deal of concern over the safety of commercial trucks, caused by their greatly increased role in serious accidents since federal deregulation in 1981.
   II. Recently, 60 percent of trucks in New York and Connecticut and 70 percent of trucks in Maryland randomly stopped by state troopers failed safety inspections.
   III. Sixteen states in the United States require no training at all for truck drivers.

   A. Since federal deregulation in 1981, there has been a great deal of concern over the safety of commercial trucks, and their greatly increased role in serious accidents. Recently, 60 percent of trucks in New York and Connecticut, and 70 percent of trucks in Maryland failed safety inspections. Sixteen states in the United States require no training at all for truck drivers.
   B. There is a great deal of concern over the safety of commercial trucks since federal deregulation in 1981. Their role in serious accidents has greatly increased. Recently, 60 percent of trucks randomly stopped in Connecticut and New York, and 70 percent in Maryland failed safety inspections conducted by state troopers. Sixteen states in the United States provide no training at all for truck drivers.
   C. Commercial trucks have a greatly increased role in serious accidents since federal deregulation in 1981. This has led to a great deal of concern. Recently, 70 percent of trucks in Maryland and 60 percent of trucks in New York and Connecticut failed inspection of those that were randomly stopped by state troopers. Sixteen states in the United States require no training for all truck drivers.
   D. Since federal deregulation in 1981, the role that commercial trucks have played in serious accidents has greatly increased, and this has led to a great deal of concern. Recently, 60 percent of trucks in New York and Connecticut, and 70 percent of trucks in Maryland randomly stopped by state troopers failed safety inspections. Sixteen states in the U.S. don't require any training for truck drivers.

8.____

9. I. No matter how much some people have, they still feel unsatisfied and want more, or want to keep what they have forever.
   II. One recent television documentary showed several people flying from New York to Paris for a one-day shopping spree to buy platinum earrings, because they were bored.
   III. In Brazil, some people are ordering coffins that cost a minimum of $45,000 and are equipping them with deluxe stereos, televisions and other graveyard necessities.

   A. Some people, despite having a great deal, still feel unsatisfied and want more, or think they can keep what they have forever. One recent documentary on television showed several people enroute from Paris to New York for a one day shopping spree to buy platinum earrings, because they were bored. Some people in Brazil are even ordering coffins equipped with such graveyard necessities as deluxe stereos and televisions. The price of the coffins start at $45,000.
   B. No matter how much some people have, they may feel unsatisfied. This leads them to want more, or to want to keep what they have forever. Recently, a television documentary depicting several people flying from New York to Paris for a one day shopping spree to buy platinum earrings. They were bored. Some people in Brazil are ordering coffins that cost at least $45,000 and come equipped with deluxe televisions, stereos and other necessary graveyard items.
   C. Some people will be dissatisfied no matter how much they have. They may want more, or they may want to keep what they have forever. One recent television documentary showed several people, motivated by boredom, jetting from New York to

9.____

Paris for a one-day shopping spree to buy platinum earrings. In Brazil, some people are ordering coffins equipped with deluxe stereos, televisions and other graveyard necessities. The minimum price for these coffins - $45,000.

D. Some people are never satisfied. No matter how much they have they still want more, or think they can keep what they have forever. One television documentary recently showed several people flying from New York to Paris for the day to buy platinum earrings because they were bored. In Brazil, some people are ordering coffins that cost $45,000 and are equipped with deluxe stereos, televisions and other graveyard necessities.

10.
   I. A television signal or Video signal has three parts.
   II. Its parts are the black-and-white portion, the color portion, and the synchronizing (sync) pulses, which keep the picture stable.
   III. Each video source, whether it's a camera or a video-cassette recorder, contains its own generator of these synchronizing pulses to accompany the picture that it's sending in order to keep it steady and straight.
   IV. In order to produce a clean recording, a video-cassette recorder must "lock-up" to the sync pulses that are part of the video it is trying to record, and this effort may be very noticeable if the device does not have genlock.

   A. There are three parts to a television or video signal: the black-and-white part, the color part, and the synchronizing (sync) pulses, which keep the picture stable. Whether it's a video-cassette recorder or a camera, each each video source contains its own pulse that synchronizes and generates the picture it's sending in order to keep it straight and steady. A video-cassette recorder must "lock up" to the sync pulses that are part of the video it's trying to record. If the device doesn't have genlock, this effort must be very noticeable.
   B. A video signal or television is comprised of three parts: the black-and-white portion, the color portion, and the the sync (synchronizing) pulses, which keep the picture stable. Whether it's a camera or a video-cassette recorder, each video source contains its own generator of these synchronizing pulses. These accompany the picture that it's sending in order to keep it straight and steady. A video-cassette recorder must "lock up" to the sync pulses that are part of the video it is trying to record in order to produce a clean recording. This effort may be very noticeable if the device does not have genlock.
   C. There are three parts to a television or video signal: the color portion, the black-and-white portion, and the sync (synchronizing pulses). These keep the picture stable. Each video source, whether it's a video-cassette recorder or a camera, generates these synchronizing pulses accompanying the picture it's sending in order to keep it straight and steady. If a clean recording is to be produced, a video-cassette recorder must store the sync pulses that are part of the video it is trying to record. This effort may not be noticeable if the device does not have genlock.
   D. A television signal or video signal has three parts: the black-and-white portion, the color portion, and the synchronizing (sync) pulses. It's the sync pulses which keep the picture stable, which accompany it and keep it steady and straight. Whether it's a camera or a video-cassette recorder, each video source contains its own generator of these synchronizing pulses. To produce a clean recording, a video-cassette recorder must "lock-up" to the sync pulses that are part of the video it is trying to record. If the device does not have genlock, this effort may be very noticeable.

KEY (CORRECT ANSWERS)

1. C
2. B
3. A
4. B
5. D

6. A
7. B
8. D
9. C
10. D

SUPERVISION STUDY GUIDE

Social science has developed information about groups and leadership in general and supervisor-employee relationships in particular. Since organizational effectiveness is closely linked to the ability of supervisors to direct the activities of employees, these findings are important to executives everywhere.

IS A SUPERVISOR A LEADER?

First-line supervisors are found in all large business and government organizations. They are the men at the base of an organizational hierarchy. Decisions made by the head of the organization reach them through a network of intermediate positions. They are frequently referred to as part of the management team, but their duties seldom seem to support this description.

A supervisor of clerks, tax collectors, meat inspectors, or securities analysts is not charged with budget preparation. He cannot hire or fire the employees in his own unit on his say-so. He does not administer programs which require great planning, coordinating, or decision making.

Then what is he? He is the man who is directly in charge of a group of employees doing productive work for a business or government agency. If the work requires the use of machines, the men he supervises operate them. If the work requires the writing of reports, the men he supervises write them. He is expected to maintain a productive flow of work without creating problems which higher levels of management must solve. But is he a leader?

To carry out a specific part of an agency's mission, management creates a unit, staffs it with a group of employees and designates a supervisor to take charge of them. Management directs what this unit shall do, from time to time changes directions, and often indicates what the group should not do. Management presumably creates status for the supervisor by giving him more pay, a title, and special priviledges.

Management asks a supervisor to get his workers to attain organizational goals, including the desired quantity and quality of production. Supposedly, he has authority to enable him to achieve this objective. Management at least assumes that by establishing the status of the supervisor's position it has created sufficient authority to enable him to achieve these goals -- not his goals, nor necessarily the group's, but management's goals.

In addition, supervision includes writing reports, keeping records of membership in a higher-level administrative group, industrial engineering, safety engineering, editorial duties, housekeeping duties, etc. The supervisor as a member of an organizational network, must be responsible to the changing demands of the management above him. At the same time, he must be responsive to the demands of the work group of which he is a member. He is placed in the difficult position of communicating and implementing new decisions, changed programs and revised production quotas for his work group, although he may have had little part in developing them.

It follows, then, that supervision has a special characteristic: achievement of goals, previously set by management, through the efforts of others. It is in this feature of the supervisor's job that we find the role of a leader in the sense of the following definition: *A leader is that person who <u>most</u> effectively influences group activities toward goal setting and goal achievements.*

This definition is broad. It covers both leaders in groups that come together voluntarily and in those brought together through a work assignment in a factory, store, or government agency. In the natural group, the authority necessary to attain goals is determined by the group membership and is granted by them. In the working group, it is apparent that the establishment of a supervisory position creates a predisposition on the part of employees to accept the authority of the occupant of that position. We cannot, however, assume that mere occupancy confers authority sufficient to assure the accomplishment of an organization's goals.

Supervision is different, then, from leadership. The supervisor is expected to fulfill the role of leader but without obtaining a grant of authority from the group he supervises. The supervisor is expected to influence the group in the achieving of goals but is often handicapped by having little influence on the organizational process by which goals are set. The supervisor, because he works in an organizational setting, has the burdens of additional organizational duties and restrictions and requirements arising out of the fact that his position is subordinate to a hierarchy of higher-level supervisors. These differences between leadership and supervision are reflected in our definition: *Supervision is basically a leadership role, in a formal organization, which has as its objective the effective influencing of other employees.*

Even though these differences between supervision and leadership exist, a significant finding of experimenters in this field is that supervisors <u>must</u> be leaders to be successful.

The problem is: How can a supervisor exercise leadership in an organizational setting? We might say that the supervisor is expected to be a natural leader in a situation which does not come about naturally. His situation becomes really difficult in an organization which is more eager to make its supervisors into followers rather than leaders.

LEADERSHIP: NATURAL AND ORGANIZATIONAL

Leadership, in its usual sense of *natural* leadership, and supervision are not the same. In some cases, leadership embraces broader powers and functions than supervision; in other cases, supervision embraces more than leadership. This is true both because of the organization and technical aspects of the supervisor's job and because of the relatively freer setting and inherent authority of the natural leader.

The natural leader usually has much more authority and influence than the supervisor. Group members not only follow his command but prefer it that way. The employee, however, can appeal the supervisor's commands to his union or to the supervisor's superior or to the personnel office. These intercessors represent restrictions on the supervisor's power to lead.

The natural leader can gain greater membership involvement in the group's objectives, and he can change the objectives of the group. The supervisor can attempt to gain employee support only for management's objectives; he cannot set other objectives. In these instances leadership is broader than supervision.

The natural leader must depend upon whatever skills are available when seeking to attain objectives. The supervisor is trained in the administrative skills necessary to achieve management's goals. If he does not possess the requisite skills, however, he can call upon management's technicians.

A natural leader can maintain his leadership, in certain groups, merely by satisfying members' need for group affilation. The supervisor must maintain his leadership by directing and organizing his group to achieve specific organizational goals set for him and his group by management. He must have a technical competence and a kind of coordinating ability which is not needed by many natural leaders.

A natural leader is responsible only to his group which grants him authority. The supervisor is responsible to management, which employs him, and, also, to the work group of which he is a member. The supervisor has the exceedingly difficult job of reconciling the demands of two groups frequently in conflict. He is often placed in the untenable position of trying to play two antagonisic roles. In the above instances, supervision is broader than leadership.

ORGANIZATIONAL INFLUENCES ON LEADERSHIP

The supervisor is both a product and a prisoner of the organization wherein we find him. The organization which creates the supervisor's position also obstructs, restricts, and channelizes the exercise of his duties. These influences extend beyond prescribed functional relationships to specific supervisory behavior. For example, even in a face-to-face situation involving one of his subordinates, the supervisor's actions are controlled to a great extent by his organization. His behavior must conform to the organization policy on human relations, rules which dictate personnel procedures, specific prohibitions governing conduct, the attitudes of his own superior, etc. He is not a free agent operating within the limits of his work group. His freedom of action is much more circumscribed than is generally admitted. The organizational influences which limit his leadership actions can be classified as structure, prescriptions, and proscriptions.

The organizational structure places each supervisor's position in context with other designated positions. It determines the relationships between his position and specific positions which impinge on his. The structure of the organization designates a certain position to which he looks for orders and information about his work. It gives a particular status to his position within a pattern of statuses from which he perceives that (1) certain positions are on a par, organizationally, with his, (2) other positions are subordinate, and (3) still others are superior. The organizational structure determines those positions to which he should look for advice and assistance, and those positions to which he should give advice and assistance.

For instance, the organizational structure has predetermined that the supervisor of a clerical processing unit shall report to a supervisory position in a higher echelon. He shall have certain relationships with the supervisors of the work units which transmit work to and receive work from his unit. He shall discuss changes and clarification of procedures with certain staff units, such as organization and methods, cost accounting, and personnel. He shall consult supervisors of units which provide or receive special work assignments.

The organizational structure, however, establishes patterns other than those of the relationships of positions. These are the patterns of responsibility, authority, and expectations.

The supervisor is responsible for certain activities or results; he is presumably invested with the authority to achieve these. His set of authority and responsibility is interwoven with other sets to the end that all goals and functions of the organization are parceled out in small, manageable lots. This, of course, establishes a series of expectations: a single supervisor can perform his particular set of duties only upon the assumption that preceding or contiguous sets of duties have been, or are being, carried out. At the same time, he is aware of the expectations of others that he will fulfill his functional role.

The structure of an organization establishes relationships between specified positions and specific expectations for these positions. The fact that these relationships and expectations are established is one thing; whether or not they are met is another.

PRESCRIPTIONS AND PROSCRIPTIONS

But let us return to the organizational influences which act to restrict the supervisor's exercise of leadership. These are the prescriptions and proscriptions generally in effect in all organizations, and those peculiar to a single organization. In brief these are the *thous shalt's* and the *thou shalt not's*.

Organizations not only prescribe certain duties for individual supervisory positions, they also prescribe specific methods and means of carrying out these duties and maintaining management-employee relations. These include rules, regulations, policy, and. tradition. It does no good for the supervisor to say, *This seems to be the best way to handle such-and such,* if the organization has established a routine for dealing with problems. For good or bad, there are rules that state that firings shall be executed in such a manner, accompanied by a certain notification; that training shall be conducted, and in this manner. Proscriptions are merely negative prescriptions: you may not discriminate against any employee because of politics or race; you shall not suspend any employee without following certain procedures and obtaining certain approvals.

Most of these prohibitions and rules apply to the area of interpersonal relations, precisely the area which is now arousing most interest on the part of administrators and managers. We have become concerned about the contrast between formally prescribed relationships and interpersonal relationships, and this brings us to the often discussed informal organization.

FORMAL AND INFORMAL ORGANIZATIONS

As we well know, the functions and activities of any organization are broken down into individual units of work called positions. Administrators must establish a pattern which will link these positions to each other and relate them to a system of authority and responsibility. Man-to-man are spelled out as plainly as possible for all to understand. Managers, then, build an official structure which we call the formal organization.

In these same organizations employees react individually and in groups to institutionally determined roles. John, a worker, rides in the same car pool as Joe, a foreman. An unplanned communication develops. Harry, a machinist, knows more about highspeed machining than his foreman or anyone else in his shop. An unofficial tool boss comes into being. Mary, who fought with Jane is promoted over her. Jane now ignores Mary's directions. A planned relationship fails to develop. The employees have built a structure which we call the informal organization.

Formal organization is a system of management-prescribed relations between positions in an organization.

Informal organization is a network of unofficial relations between people in an organization.

These definitions might lead us to the absurd conclusion that positions carry out formal activities and that employees spend their time in unofficial activities. We must recognize that organizational activities are in all cases carried out by people. The formal structure provides a needed framework within which interpersonal relations occur. What we call informal organization is the complex of normal, natural relations among employees. These personal relationships may be negative or positive. That is, they may impede or aid the achievement of organizational, goals. For example, friendship between two supervisors greatly increases the probability of good cooperation and coordination between their sections. On the other hand, *buck passing* nullifies the formal structure by failure to meet a prescribed and expected responsibility.

It is improbable that an ideal organization exists where all activities are acarried out in strict conformity to a formally prescribed pattern of functional roles. Informal organization arises because of the incompleteness and ambiguities in the network of formally prescribed relationships, or in response to the needs or inadequacies of supervisors or managers who hold prescribed functional roles in an organization. Many of these relationships are not prescribed by the organizational pattern; many cannot be prescribed; many should not be prescribed.

Management faces the problem of keeping the informal organization in harmony with the mission of the agency. One way to do this is to make sure that all employees have a clear understanding of and are sympathetic with that mission. The issuance of organizational charts, procedural manuals, and functional descriptions of the work to be done by divisions and sections helps communicate management's plans and goals. Issuances alone, of course, cannot do the whole job. They should be accompanied by oral discussion and explanation. Management must ensure that there is mutual understanding and acceptance of charts and procedures. More important is that management acquaint itself with the attitudes, activities, and peculiar brands of logic which govern the informal organization. Only through this type of knowledge can they and supervisors keep informal goals consistent with the agency mission.

SUPERVISION, STATUS, AND FUNCTIONAL ROLE

A well-established supervisor is respected by the employees who work with him. They defer to his wishes. It is clear that a superior-subordinate relationship has been established. That is, status of the supervisor has been established in relation to other employees of the same work group. This same supervisor gains the respect of employees when he behaves in a certain manner. He will be expected generally, to follow the customs of the group in such matters as dress, recreation, and manner of speaking. The group has a set of expectations as to his behavior. His position is a functional role which carries with it a collection of rights and obligations.

The position of supervisor usually has a status distinct from the individual who occupies it: it is much like a position description which exists whether or not there is an incumbent. The status of a supervisory position is valued higher than that of an employee position both because of the functional role of leadership which is assigned to it and because of the status symbols of titles, rights, and privileges which go with it.

Social ranking, or status, is not simple because it involves both the position and the man. An individual may be ranked higher than others because of his education, social background, perceived leadership ability, or conformity to group customs and ideals. If such a man is ranked higher by the members of a work group than their supervisor, the supervisor's effectiveness may be seriously undermined.

If the organization does not build and reinforce a supervisor's status, his position can be undermined in a different way. This will happen when managers go around rather than through the supervisor or designate him as a straw boss, acting boss, or otherwise not a real boss.

Let us clarify this last point. A role, and corresponding status, establishes a set of expectations. Employees expect their supervisor to do certain things and to act in certain ways. They are prepared to respond to that expected behavior. When the supervisor's behavior does not conform to their expectations, they are surprised, confused, and ill-at-ease. It becomes necessary for them to resolve their confusion, if they can. They might do this by turning to one of their own members for leadership. If the confusion continues, or their attempted solutions are not satisfactory, they will probably become a poorly motivated, non-cohesive group which cannot function very well.

COMMUNICATION AND THE SUPERVISOR

In a recent survey railroad workers reported that they rarely look to their supervisors for information about the company. This is startling, at least to us, because we ordinarily think of the supervisor as the link between management and worker. We expect the supervisor to be the prime source of information about the company. Actually, the railroad workers listed the supervisor next to last in the order of their sources of information. Most suprising of all, the supervisors, themselves, stated that rumor and unofficial contacts were their principal sources of information. Here we see one of the reasons why supervisors may not be as effective as management desires.

The supervisor is not only being bypassed by his work group, he is being ignored, and his position weakened, by the very organization which is holding him responsible for the activities of his workers. If he is management's representative to the employee, then management has an obligation to keep him informed of its activities. This is necessary if he is to carry out his functions efficiently and maintain his leadership in the work group. The supervisor is expected to be a source of information; when he is not, his status is not clear, and employees are dissatisfied because he has not lived up to expectations.

By providing information to the supervisor to pass along to employees, we can strengthen his position as leader of the group, and increase satisfaction and cohesion within the group. Because he has more information than the other members, receives information sooner, and passes it along at the proper times, members turn to him as a source and also provide him with information in the hope of receiving some in return. From this we can see an increase in group cohesiveness because:

- Employees are bound closer to their supervisor because he is *in the know*
- there is less need to go outside the group for answers
- employees will more quickly turn to the supervisor for enlightenment.

The fact that he has the answers will also enhance the supervisor's standing in the eyes of his men. This increased sta,tus will serve to bolster his authority and control of the group and will probably result in improved morale and productivity.

The foregoing, of course, does not mean that all management information should be given out. There are obviously certain policy determinations and discussions which need not or cannot be transmitted to all supervisors. However, the supervisor must be kept as fully informed as possible so that he can answer questions when asked and can allay needless fears and anxieties. Further, the supervisor has the responsibility of encouraging employee questions and submissions of information. He must be able to present information to employees so that it is clearly understood and accepted. His attitude and manner should make it clear that he believes in what he is saying, that the information is necessary or desirable to the group, and that he is prepared to act on the basis of the information.

SUPERVISION AND JOB PERFORMANCE

The productivity of work groups is a product; employees' efforts are multiplied by the supervision they receive. Many investigators have analyzed this relationship and have discovered elements of supervision which differentiate high and low production groups. These researchers have identified certain types of supervisory practices which they classify as *employee-centered* and other types which they classify as *production centered*.

The difference between these two kinds of supervision lies not in specific practices but in the approach or orientation to supervision. The employee-centered supervisor directs most of his efforts toward increasing employee motivation. He is concerned more with realizing the potential energy of persons than with administrative and technological methods of increasing efficiency and productivity. He is the man who finds ways of causing employees to want to work harder with the same tools. These supervisors emphasize the personal relations between their employees and themselves.

Now, obviously, these pictures are overdrawn. No one supervisor has all the virtues of the ideal type of employee-centered supervisor. And, fortunately, no one supervisor has all the bad traits found in many production-centered supervisors. We should remember that the various practices that researchers have found which distinguish these two kinds of supervision represent the many practices and methods of supervisors of all gradations between these extremes. We should be careful, too, of the implications of the labels attached to the two types. For instance, being production-centered is not necessarily bad, since the principal responsibility of any supervisor is maintaining the production level that is expected of his work group. Being employee-centered may not necessarily be good, if the only result is a happy, chuckling crew of loafers. To return to the researchers's findings, employee-centered supervisors:

- Recommend promotions, transfers, pay increases
- Inform men about what is happening in the company
- Keep men posted on how well they are doing
- Hear complaints and grievances sympathetically
- Speak up for subordinates

Production-centered supervisors, on the other hand, don't do those things. They check on employees more frequently, give more detailed and frequent instructions, don't give reasons for changes, and are more punitive when mistakes are made. Employee-centered supervisors were reported to contribute to high morale and high production, whereas production-centered supervision was associated with lower morale and less production.

More recent findings, however, show that the relationship between supervision and productivity is not this simple. Investigators now report that high production is more frequently associated with supervisory practices which combine employee-centered behavior with concern for production. (This concern is not the same, however, as anxiety about production, which is the hallmark of our production-centered supervisor.) Let us examine these apparently contradictory findings and the premises from which they are derived.

SUPERVISION AND MORALE

Why do supervisory activities cause high or low production? As the name implies, the activities of the employee-centered supervisor tend to relate him more closely and satisfactorily to his workers. The production-centered supervisor's practices tend to separate him from his group and to foster antagonism. An analysis of this difference may answer our question.

Earlier, we pointed out that the supervisor is a type of leader and that leadership is intimately related to the group in which it occurs. We discover, now, that an employee-centered supervisor's primary activities are concerned with both his leadership and his group membership. Such a supervisor is a member of a group and occupies a leadership role in that group.

These facts are sometimes obscured when we speak of the supervisor as management's representative, or as the organizational link between management and the employee, or as the end of the chain of command. If we really want to understand what it is we expect of the supervisor, we must remember that he is the designated leader of a group of employees to whom he is bound by interaction and interdependence.

Most of his actions are aimed, consciously or unconsciously, at strengthening membership ties in the group. This includes both making members more conscious that he is a member of their grout) and causing members to identify themselves more closely with the group. These ends are accomplished by:

> making the group more attractive to the worker: they
>> find satisfaction of their needs for recognition,
>> friendship, enjoyable work, etc.;
>
> maintaining open communication: employees can express
>> their views and obtain information about the organization.
>
> giving assistance: members can seek advice on
>> personal problems as well as their work; and
>
> acting as a buffer between the group and management:
>> he speaks up for his men and explains the reasons
>> for management's decisions.

Such actions both strengthen group cohesiveness and solidarity and affirm the supervisor's leadership position in the group.

DEFINING MORALE

This brings us back to a point mentioned earlier. We had said that employee-centered supervisors contribute to high morale as well as to high production. But how can we explain units which have low morale and high productivity, or vice versa? Usually production and morale are considered separately, partly because they are measured against different criteria and partly because, in some instances, they seem to be independent of each other.

Some of this difficulty may stem from confusion over definitions of morale. Morale has been defined as, or measured by, absences from work, satisfaction with job or company, dissension among members of work groups, productivity, apathy or lack of interest, readiness to help others, and a general aura of happiness as rated by observers. Some of these criteria of morale are not subject to the influence of the supervisor, and some of them are not clearly related to productivity. Definitions like these invite findings of low morale coupled with high production.

Both productivity and morale can be influenced by environmental factors not under the control of group members or supervisors. Such things as plant layout, organizational structure and goals, lighting, ventilation, communications, and management planning may have an adverse or desirable effect.

We might resolve the dilemma by defining morale on the basis of our understanding of the supervisor as leader of a group; morale is the degree of satisfaction of group members with their leadership. In this light, the supervisor's employee-centered activities bear a clear relation to morale. His efforts to increase employee identification with the group and to strengthen his leadership lead to greater satisfaction with that leadership. By increasing group cohesiveness and by demonstrating that his influence and power can aid the group, he is able to enhance his leadership status and afford satisfaction to the group.

SUPERVISION, PRODUCTION, AND MORALE

There are factors within the organization itself which determine whether increased production is possible:

Are production goals expressed in terms understandable to employees and are they realistic?

Do supervisors responsible for production respect the agency mission and production goals?

If employees do not know how to do the job well, does management provide a trainer--often the supervisor--who can teach efficient work methods?

There are other factors within the work group which determine whether increased production will be attained:

Is leadership present which can bring about the desired level of production?

Are production goals accepted by employees as reasonable and attainable?

If group effort is involved, are members able to coordinate their efforts?

Research findings confirm the view that an employee-centered supervisor can achieve higher morale than a production-centered supervisor. Managers may well ask what is the relationship between this and production?

Supervision is production-oriented to the extent that it focuses attention on achieving organizational goals, and plans and devises methods for attaining them; it is employee-centered to the extent that it focuses attention on employee attitudes toward those goals, and plans and works toward maintenance of employee satisfaction.

High productivity and low morale result when a supervisor plans and organizes work efficiently but cannot achieve high membership satisfaction. Low production and high morale result when a supervisor, though keeping members satisfied with his leadership, either has not gained acceptance of organizational goals or does not have the technical competence to achieve them.

The relationship between supervision, morale, and productivity is an interdependent one, with the supervisor playing an integrating role due to his ability to influence productivity and morale independently of each other.

A supervisor who can plan his work well has good technical knowledge, and who can install better production methods can raise production without necessarily increasing group satisfaction. On the other hand, a supervisor who can motivate his employees and keep them satisfied with his leadership can gain high production in spite of technical difficulties and environmental obstacles.

CLIMATE AND SUPERVISION

Climate, the intangible environment of an organization made up of attitudes, beliefs, and traditions, plays a large part in morale, productivity, and supervision. Usually when we speak of climate and its relationship to morale and productivity, we talk about the merits of *democratic* versus *authoritarian* climate. Employees seem to produce more and have higher morale in a democratic climate, whereas in an authoritarian climate, the reverse seems to be true or so the researchers tell us. We would do well to determine what these terms mean to supervision.

Perhaps most of our difficulty in understanding and applying these concepts comes from our emotional reactions to the words themselves. For example, authoritarian climate is usually painted as the very blackest kind of dictatorship. This not surprising, because we are usually expected to believe that it is invariably bad. Conversely, democratic climate is drawn to make the driven snow look impure by comparison.

Now these descriptions are most probably true when we talk about our political processes, or town meetings, or freedom of speech. However the same labels have been used by social scientists in other contexts and have also been applied to government and business organizations, without, it seems, any recognition that the meanings and their social values may have changed somewhat .

For example, these labels were used in experiments conducted in an informal class room setting using 11 year old boys as subjects. The descriptive labels applied to the climate of the setting as well as the type of leadership practiced. When these labels were transferred to a management setting it seems that many presumed that they principally meant the king of leadership rather than climate. We can see that there is a great difference between the experimental and management settings and that leadership practices for one might be inappropriate for the other.

It is doubtful that formal work organizations can be anything but authoritarian, in that goals are set by management and a hierarchy exists through which decisions and orders from the top are transmitted downward. Organizations are authoritarian by structure and need: direction and control are placed in the hands of a few in order to gain fast and efficient decision making. Now this does not mean to describe a dictatorship. It is merely the recognition of the fact that direction of organizational affairs comes from above. It should be noted that leadership in some natural groups is, in this sense, authoritarian.

Granting that formal organizations have this kind of authoritarian leadership, can there be a democratic climate? Certainly there can be, but we would want to define and delimit this term. A more realistic meaning of democratic climate in organizations is, the use of permissive and participatory methods in management-employee relations. That is, a mutual exchange of information and explanation with the granting of individual freedom within certain restricted and defined limits. However, it is not our purpose to debate the merits of authoritarianism versus democracy. We recognize that within the small work group there is a need for freedom from constraint and an increase in participation in order to achieve organizational goals within the framework of the organizational environment.

Another aspect of climate is best expressed by this familiar, and true saying: actions speak louder than words. Of particular concern to us is this effect of management climate on the behavior of supervisors, particularly in employee-centered activities.

There have been reports of disappointment with efforts to make supervisors more employee-centered. Managers state that, since research has shown ways of improving human relations, supervisors should begin to practice these methods. Usually a training course in human relations is established, and supervisors are given this training. Managers then sit back and wait for the expected improvements, only to find that there are none.

If we wish to produce changes in the supervisor's behavior, the climate must be made appropriate and rewarding to the changed behavior. This means that top-level attitudes and behavior cannot deny or contradict the change we are attempting to effect. Basic changes in organizational behavior cannot be made with any permanence, unless we provide an environment that is receptive to the changes and rewards those persons who do change.

IMPROVING SUPERVISION

Anyone who has read this far might expect to find *A Dozen Rules for Dealing With Employees* or *29 Steps to Supervisory Success.* We will not provide such a list.

Simple rules suffer from their simplicity. They ignore the complexities of human behavior. Reliance upon rules may cause supervisors to concentrate on superficial aspects of their relations with employees. It may preclude genuine understanding.

The supervisor who relies on a list of rules tends to think of people in mechanistic terms. In a certain situation, he uses *Rule No. 3.* Employees are not treated as thinking and feeling persons, but rather as figures in a formula: Rule 3 applied to employee X = Production.

Employees usually recognize mechanical manipulation and become dissatisfied and resentful. They lose faith in, and respect for, their supervisor, and this may be reflected in lower morale and productivity.

We do not mean that supervisors must become social science experts if they wish to improve. Reports of current research indicate that there are two major parts of their job which can be strengthened through self-improvement: (1) Work planning, including technical skills. (2) Motivation of employees.

The most effective supervisors combine excellence in the administrative and technical aspects of their work with friendly and considerate personal relations with their employees.

CRITICAL PERSONAL RELATIONS

Later in this chaper we shall talk about administrative aspects of supervision, but first let us comment on *friendly and considerate personal relations*. We have discussed this subject throughout the preceding chapters, but we want to review some of the critical supervisory influences on personal relations.

Closeness of Supervision

The closeness of supervision has an important effect on productivity and morale. Mann and Dent found that supervisors of low-producing units supervise very closely, while high-producing supervisors exercise only general supervision. It was found that the low-producing supervisors:

- check on employees more frequently
- give more detailed and frequent instructions
- limit employee's freedom to do job in own way.

Workers who felt less closely supervised reported that they were better satisfied with their jobs and the company. We should note that the manner or attitude of the supervisor has an important bearing on whether employees perceive supervision as being close or general.

These findings are another way of saying that supervision does not mean standing over the employee and telling him what to do and when and how to do it. The more effective supervisor tells his employees what is required, giving general instructions.

COMMUNICATION

Supervisors of high-production units consider communication as one of the most important aspects of their job. Effective communication is used by these supervisors to achieve better interpersonal relations and improved employee motivation. Low-production supervisors do not rate communication as highly important.

High-producing supervisors find that an important aid to more effective communication is listening. They are ready to listen to both personal problems or interests and questions about the work. This does not mean that they are *nosey* or meddle in their employees' personal lives, but rather that they show a willingness to listen, and do listen, if their employees wish to discuss problems.

These supervisors inform employees about forthcoming changes in work; they discuss agency policy with employees; and they make sure that each employee knows how well he is doing. What these supervisors do is use two-way communication effectively. Unless the supervisor freely imparts information, he will not receive information in return.

Attitudes and perception are frequently affected by communication or the lack of it. Research surveys reveal that many supervisors are not aware of their employees' attitudes, nor do they know what personal reactions their supervision arouses. Through frank discussions with employees, they have been surprised to discover employee beliefs about which they were ignorant. Discussion sometimes reveals that the supervisor and his employees have totally different impressions about the same event. The supervisor should be constantly on the alert for misconceptions about his words and deeds. He must remember that, although his actions are perfectly clear to himself, they may be, and frequently are, viewed differently by employees.

Failure to communicate information results in misconceptions and false assumptions. What you say and how you say it will strongly affect your employees' attitudes and perceptions. By giving them available information you can prevent misconceptions; by discussion, you may be able to change attitudes; by questioning; you can discover what the perceptions and assumptions really are. And it need hardly be added that actions should conform very closely to words.

If we were to attempt to reduce the above discussion on communication to rules, we would have a long list which would be based on one cardinal principle: Don't make assumptions!

- o Don't assume that your employees know; tell them.
- o Don't assume that you know how they feel; find out.
- o Don't assume that they understand; clarify.

20 SUPERVISORY HINTS

1. Avoid inconsistency.
2. Always give employees a chance to explain their actions before taking disciplinary action. Don't allow too much time for a "cooling off" period before disciplining an employee.
3. Be specific in your criticisms.
4. Delegate responsibility wisely.
5. Do not argue or lose your temper, and avoid being impatient.
6. Promote mutual respect and be fair, impartial and open-minded.
7. Keep in mind that asking for employees' advice and input can be helpful in decision making.
8. If you make promises, keep them.
9. Always keep the feelings, abilities, dignity and motives of your staff in mind.
10. Remain loyal to your employees' interests.
11. Never criticize employees in front of others, or treat employees like children.
12. Admit mistakes. Don't place blame on your employees, or make excuses.
13. Be reasonable in your expectations, give complete instructions, and establish well-planned goals.
14. Be knowledgeable about office details and procedures, but avoid becoming bogged down in details.
15. Avoid supervising too closely or too loosely. Employees should also view you as an approachable supervisor.
16. Remember that employees' personal problems may affect job performance, but become involved only when appropriate.
17. Work to develop workers, and to instill a feeling of cooperation while working toward mutual goals.
18. Do not overpraise or underpraise, be properly appreciative.
19. Never ask an employee to discipline someone for you.
20. A complaint, even if unjustified, should be taken seriously.